40 Considerables

A Little Purple Book to Help You Navigate
Life's Gray Areas & Live More Colorfully

by
Richard Krevolin

40 Considerables
*A Little Purple Book to Help You Navigate Life's
Gray Areas & Live More Colorfully*

NOTE: The strategies and insights contained herein
are solely based on the author's own experiences and
intended to offer inspiration and, dare I say, a bit of
life guidance. If you feel like you are struggling, please
consult with a mental health care professional.

ISBN: 978-0-9905893-9-6

First Edition

Publisher: Mystery House Publishing, Inc.
Power Story, LLC
Cover Design: Fab Bozzolo

Author Richard Krevolin can be reached at:
RKrevolin@yahoo.com,
KrevolinArtsFoundation.com

Printed in the United States of America

Table of Contents

FOREWORD by Irwin Kula

As you read this book, don't be surprised to find yourself nodding in agreement with many of the suggestions that the author offers. And yet, while agreeing with these suggestions, you may also have a gnawing feeling that comes with not living out—not "witnessing" if you will—these "obvious" pieces of wisdom about life. How is it we can shake our head yes, of course, each insight in this little book is right and wise and yet, at the same time, we are still not living our life according to these precepts?

That is because this book is filled with concepts which at first glance may seem like you already know them or that they are so simple that you can easily dismiss them but, as the author says, familiar and simple doesn't necessarily mean easy to implement.

I hope this book may remind you in novel and personal ways of how to live some basic truths as well as evoking and stimulating the mysterious questions of why we so often don't act in light of what we know to be the truth.

I believe this dichotomy, this paradox if you will, is an ancient human conundrum. In one of the most quoted verses in Scripture, Paul laments, "I do not understand what I do. For what I want to do I do not do, but what I hate I do." Contemporary psychologists call this the "intention-action gap," also known as the "value-action gap" or "knowledge-attitudes-practice gap." It is the experience we all know well when our values, attitudes, or intentions don't match our actions.

And so, as you read this book, please consider the idea of having—and particularly allowing, perhaps even welcoming—your own visceral/kinesthetic/sensory experience and the idea that discomfiting experiences must be felt to help us grow and change.

Many of the personal stories in this book are not simply to "prove" the wisdom of the suggestions but also to lift up the difficult and sometimes painful process of narrowing the gap between attitude, intention, and action.

There are so many reasons for this gap. We have a behavioral bias favoring immediate gratification, so be on the lookout for how often integrating an obvious piece of wisdom that would benefit you comes with a need for delayed gratification.

Sometimes the intention-action gap comes from being too ambitious, as we want to swallow the wisdom down and act upon it in one fell swoop. If you feel that gnawing gap reading one of the suggestions in this book, don't try to suddenly change completely. Take it one incremental step at a time, as transformation is the consequence of myriad small changes. In other words, as the author suggests, you may want to chew on them instead of reading all at once.

Sometimes we choose to do the "right" thing, but something about our environment can stop us from carrying it out. Most interestingly, we human beings do not change our behavior because someone tells us what we must do to fix ourselves. In fact, recent studies show that telling people how they are wrong and how we think they should improve actually hinders learning!

Our best shot at narrowing the attitude-intention-action gap is when people who know us and care about us tell us what they experience and what they feel. And we also know that the degree to which we believe we can control an outcome will influence our willingness to engage in the change, hence the author's occasionally repeated mentions that with all of these ideas it's your choice whether or not to implement them.

So, as you read the suggestions offered in this book, here is my take on them. The author is not trying to fix you. He is merely sharing what he feels, what he has experienced, and what has worked for him. If you feel the sense of a gnawing gap in between your agreement with the ideas in this book and your genuine desire to change your behavior and your actions, don't fight it, don't deny or ignore it—embrace the messiness.

And if you do find you want to implement any or all of these into your life, please, don't try to suddenly change completely. Just take it one incremental step at a time (that adage is oft repeated for a reason), as transformation is the consequence of myriad small changes. Be ready to delay gratification just a bit, as long-term gain in human flourishing always comes with some short-term discomfort.

And know that at least regarding the suggestions in this book, YOU do indeed control the outcome.

In the end, this book makes a humble claim about stuff the author has learned—in the inevitable hard and circuitous way—about how to have a better life, since these concepts have been so instrumental in the author's own transformation.

In doing so, it reflects a hope that as you read this, you will feel you already know this stuff—or at least a lot of it—and you will recognize the wisdom of it. And then you will go on to realize, hmmm… It feels so true and yet, at the same time, so difficult to embody. That is the challenge, the gift, and the beauty of this offering.

EDITOR'S NOTE

Not Rules, but "Considerables"

Life is for living. Such is the reminder in this quote attributed to Robert DeNiro: "You'll have time to rest when you're dead." It's a quote this book's author, Richard Krevolin, has been known to say a time or three as well. Rich has a penchant for pursuing multiple interests and tends to be in constant motion. In fact, I refer to him as "The Hummingbird," since his pace seems similar to the constant motion of that creature who moves so quickly that it hums as it travels to feed on life's sweet nectar.

The jobs and passions Rich has explored in under six decades have included professor, playwright, book author, filmmaker and documentarian, director, farmer, storytelling consultant, art teacher, painter, runner, tennis player, golfer, cookie jar collector... You get the idea. As much as he will say he's enjoyed facets of each, he'll also be the first to tell you that most, if not every, pursuit has involved both failures and worthwhile experiences, each with their own wake-up calls and/or lessons and/or reminders. As long as we are alive, we keep learning, and for Rich, one of the more recent insights is that sometimes it's good to slow down—at least a little—and appreciate the journey while you're on it.

When COVID hit, he actually did slow down just enough to consider, and appreciate, what kinds of lessons have made a difference in his life thus far. And in life's inevitable yin and yang, the flip-side result was the action of creating this book (after all, hummingbirds can't stop moving if they are to thrive). And since he's already begun working on developing his next project, he asked me if I'd craft this introductory note simply to share with you a few thoughts about this book.

Please note, this was not intended to be a how-to book but one that shares stories and concepts which Rich asserts have made his life and relationships feel more meaningful, enjoyable, and satisfying. He has, in another example of his ongoing creating, forged a new word for the 40 concepts included here, dubbing them "considerables." This moniker emerged from the idea of something considerable (no *s*) being "worth consideration," with the *s* added because there are 40 "bite-size sharings" in this book that he feels are well worth chewing on and contemplating to make life better. Though old habits die hard, through using these ideas he has said he no longer gets as caught up in the same conundrums, stresses, etc. as he used to, so he can expend his energy on living more fully (a fun learning for someone always on the go).

No one goes through life without some stress, struggle, or uncertainty. So, in the same way you might share information with others regarding things that changed your life for the better, Rich hopes these considerables will be as helpful to you as they've been for him and that, by putting them in book form, you now have in one place a number of ideas you can easily turn to when wanting a reminder or a fresh perspective. And hopefully, especially if they are *not* new to you, the way they are presented here will inspire you to reconsider them and implement them in new ways.

As we worked on this book, three "themes" seemed to keep recurring, which we figured would be worth mentioning at the start.

Krevolin's Considerables are ideas that are "simple but not necessarily easy": Most of these concepts, if not all, will be familiar to you. They are ideas which are simple (sometimes so simple that we take them for granted and/or dismiss their import), but they are not always easy to implement and utilize on an ongoing basis, even when we have the felt experience that they make our lives better and are well worth working toward.

Even though simple ideas may not be easy, neither do they have to be complicated. It really is just a matter of choosing and then doing them—regardless of whether yours is a hummingbird or turtle pace or even somewhere in between. Sometimes that means just slowing down, noticing, and appreciating. Other times it may mean taking some action. Since we take so much for granted and can forget some of the most basic facets of civility and connection, and since we sometimes make things harder than they are or need to be, a return to simple can be a good thing—even though that doesn't automatically mean results will be immediate or long-lasting. After all, life is a dynamic process.

Yin & Yang: Nothing works in every single situation, so we'd like to acknowledge here at the start that there will be seemingly contradictory chapters/messages. Even though Rich's lived experience and expressed belief is that *all* of these ideas are valuable and can bring positive changes into anyone's life, each has its time and place. And that is the way life is, anyway, right? Filled with dichotomies. Yin and yang. So, as you'll see, for example, there is a time for farting around without a plan (per author Kurt Vonnegut, quoted in the "Fart Around" chapter), and there's a time when organized action is necessary (as mentioned in the "Do Something with Your Life" chapter).

The Way You Respond to This Book and Your Life Really Is Up to You: Rich is who he is. And you are uniquely you. A good thing (and perhaps simultaneously a difficult thing as well) is that whether and how you implement any considerables that resonate with you at this point in your life is up to you. Though life isn't always in our control, since you *can* control how you respond to situations, you get to choose whether and what you want to integrate to make a difference in your life.

We are all works in progress as long as we are alive, and change is said to be one of the constant aspects of that journey. Hopefully these considerables and stories offer a solid platform from which you can dive in and find pleasure integrating ones that call to you. And may any frustrations from lack of immediate change be reduced in the process of actual change. To that end, Rich suggests reading this book in small doses and aiming to see these concepts with new or clear eyes. Notice what happens when you make space for what you desire and want to prioritize at this point of your life. Maybe select one or two lessons a day.

Take the time to consider and digest them. Does something about the ideas or stories resonate with you? With each idea, is it something you want to do or try right now?

The hope is that by reviewing and doing these considerables, you will uncomplicate your life enough to bring into clear focus (and be inspired to explore further) what generates for you the greatest sense of vitality and peace. You're worth it.

~ NC

INTRODUCTION

Or, Why Should Anyone Care About Etiquette Today?

Whether you love or hate golf, there's a lot to be said for its traditions and rules of etiquette. You see, there are well-established rules in golf that apply to how players are to conduct themselves. If you don't abide by these rules, you may receive a penalty or be disqualified or kicked off a course.

Good friends of mine who are avid golfers were recently playing eighteen holes when they faced a rather awkward situation. The rowdy group in front of them were smoking, drinking, and playing way too slowly. So slowly my friends seemed to be spending the entire afternoon just sitting in their carts and waiting.

Normal golf etiquette in this situation would be to let the group behind them pass through. But these people seemed oblivious to the other human beings around them. They either didn't notice my friends waiting for them or consciously ignored them, so they never indicated for my friends to pass by, nor did they respond when my friends tried to ask for permission to pass.

Finally, my friends couldn't take it any longer and—per proper golf etiquette—decided to do the right thing and just go on by them to the next hole. That way, they could enjoy their golf game in a reasonable time frame and the people in front of them could take whatever time they wanted without interruption. But the group of people—who must have been new to golfing as they, incidentally, were also not following the dress code—were perturbed as my friends drove their golf cart past them. In fact, they were so infuriated that they screamed at the moving golf cart, *"Hey, you goddamn people ain't got no et-kit!"*

It seemed kind of ironic they'd judge someone else about having "et-kit," given their behaviors and that they weren't following the rules of etiquette established for the very forum they had chosen to play in. Even though in other situations passing someone might seem rude, in this instance it was exactly what was supposed to happen for everyone to be able to enjoy their own golf game.

Many people bristle at being told how to act, but you know what? The golf course is like a microcosm of the world and shows why we have "et-kit" rules: they work. The rules apply equally to everybody on the course and are designed to avoid upset or bedlam through consideration of others, keeping the pace of play steady, and keeping the course in good shape for everyone who'll be using it. You might argue that golf is an elitist, exclusionary sport, but please note that does not apply in this case. This incident took place on a public course which was open to all and not expensive. In other words, you can devalue the rules all you want, but they have been instated because they are good for the whole—even if, at times, they might not appeal to certain individuals.

And that's the key.

Even though we may deny it, human beings need to codify behavior in order to live together more successfully. Look at how long the Ten Commandments have been a mainstay of Western civilization. It's not a fluke that humans are drawn to codes of conduct. Simply put, things like rules of etiquette clarify life, help us avoid chaos, and enable us all to live together more harmoniously. They provide guardrails for the things in life that aren't black and white and that are tricky to navigate.

Like a medical prescription that can alleviate—if not cure—what ails you, etiquette is basically prescribed social behavior that aims to ease or prevent what's harmful or destructive to society. As with much of life, though, there can be contradictions or different situations requiring different responses, and it's helpful to be aware of the context in order to understand what behavior is considered best for getting along and avoiding chaos and societal breakdown.

What do I mean? Rules of "et-kit" are used on a daily basis and offer a cohesive sense to society, yet they may be different—as seen in the golf example above—based on the context and culture. I was taught as a boy that it's polite and respectful to look people in the eyes when I speak to them, but the same behavior might be frowned upon and perceived as a sign of aggression in some cultures in Asia or the Middle East. In some countries, like India, showing up late can be a sign of one's importance and punctuality is not always a key value. In some countries, guests burping loudly following a meal is considered proper etiquette and a compliment to the host. In America and elsewhere, some people think it's okay to engage in public displays of affection, while others don't. You get the point.

At times we are so deeply absorbed in our needs as individuals or as a specific tribe (and, in some cases, the injustices committed against us in the past) that we are no longer able to see the needs of the larger whole that we are also part of or to maintain respect when people's traditions, actions, or thoughts differ from our own. Most people's lives are a mix of positive and negative experiences and interactions. And the fact is that many changes (with positive and negative sides to each) are happening in our society as well (just look at the discussions about technological advancements and the use of AI, for one). These changes are occurring quickly and we, as a culture, are struggling to keep up.

As with any period of change and growth, there will be backlash and missteps as we figure things out. In fact, many claim that we live in a more divided age than ever before. But doesn't that mean it's more necessary than ever to try to bridge the gap by sharing ways we've learned to get along and feel better about ourselves and our lives? When we unite, we can navigate the trial and error of these new times *together*, supporting each other and making it a whole helluva lot more enjoyable in the process—hence this book of "et-kit" considerables, if you will.

Now you might ask *Who the heck are* you*, Mr. Author, to say what constitutes proper "et-kit" for me or anybody else?* I can't. Nor am I trying to. I'm simply a student of the zeitgeist and a sensitive human being who's spent decades learning, observing, and writing stories, plays, and movies about the interactions, foibles, habits, and norms of our society. In that time, I've accumulated insights that have helped me navigate my own life's uncertainties and that might—hopefully—prove to be of some value to you as a fellow human.

I'm also a believer in the power of stories to change and heal our lives, and as a storyteller myself, I'm hoping that at least starting the conversations about "et-kit" considerables will be worthwhile. I see this book not as an endpoint but as more of a starting point in a larger cultural conversation. Think about it. We are all better off when we are able to share ideas about such aspects of life as how to be a better parent, worker, partner, communicator, friend. And an exchange of ideas, thoughts, customs with those who are different from us can also be powerful and awaken us to new ways of being in the world or even confirm the ones we've come to take for granted. When you engage in a civil discussion and get to share perspectives, you can confirm beliefs, change beliefs, open hearts and minds, create and deepen relationships, and simply make life more fun, meaningful, and interesting—your own and others'. Community combats aloneness. So my aim with this work is to share some of my experiences and ideas, in the hope they add to the resources (your "et-kit" toolkit, if you will) you find helpful for navigating the gray, uncertain, stress-inducing, areas of your life in order to find more meaning and fulfillment, authentic connection, and, yes, more joy too.

The ideas in this book, like newly planted seeds, are organic and will continue to grow and change, much as our culture, our world, and we as individual humans will keep doing as long as we are alive. What I hope you'll also see in the following pages is that this book is not written with an agenda, political or religious or otherwise. It merely aims in its own way to foster thought and discussion which hopefully lead to personal insights that assist you in navigating the way forward as we all try to figure things out and get along in this experiment of shared air called modern life.

P.S. You may be wondering why this book is purple. Yes, *why purple*?

Purple seemed the best color for a book about navigating and getting out from the gray areas of life, the dull, dismal, depressing, and distressing. Purple is associated with royalty and power. Additionally, in the body's chakra system—the energy system correlating to different facets of our well-being (physical, emotional, etc.)—purple symbolizes higher consciousness, inner wisdom, and vision. It also happens to be my favorite color. As a visual artist I tend to put purple in my paintings to jazz them up.

And think about it, when you combine red states and blue states, you get one big purple state. Instead of dividing us, this book aims to bring us all together— to make us more comfortable in our relationships with ourselves and each other in order to make our lives better. If you want to change any aspect of your life, from the seemingly mundane to the momentous, all of these ideas are free and doable, and it's totally up to you if and how you choose to implement them.

If nothing else, as my mother, Evelyn Krevolin, would say, taking these ideas about "et-kit" into consideration "Couldn't hurt."

Considerable #1

SEE THAT IT'S ALL AN ILLUSION

I was fortunate to be writing partners for many years with a pretty famous actor. But fame is a funny thing. When we first met, he was still a hot commodity, and every time we had a lunch meeting, people would recognize him and ask for an autograph. He was always gracious, and I finally asked him how he dealt with the constant onslaught of attention.

He laughed, looked at me, and said, "For most of my life, I wasn't famous. Now I am. Soon, I won't be again, so I'm trying to enjoy it while it lasts. My hero was Sid Caesar. For a while, everybody knew who he was, but I just had lunch with him last week and nobody recognized him. It's all an illusion. It's all fleeting. So you gotta enjoy the ride while you're on it."

I laughed and asked him to explain further.

He thought for a moment and responded, "Okay. Look. Here's the life cycle of an actor:

"Who is Joe Blow?

"Get me Joe Blow as the star of our next picture!

"Get me somebody who's a Joe Blow type.

"Get me a young Joe Blow.

"Wait a second, who *was* Joe Blow?"

I love his wisdom here. He was never full of himself. He just realized that it's all an illusion and wouldn't last forever, so he chose to enjoy the ride and take pleasure in it while it lasted. As a creative person, he knew to appreciate the illusion rather than resent it, just as one can appreciate each unique sunset even though minutes later it will be gone. And he loved his life, which made me realize the value of his words and rethink how I missed out when I got stuck in wanting things to be or stay a particular way.

This is a good way to appreciate our lives more deeply, even if we're not famous actors. If we can't change what happened yesterday (or years ago) and if what occurs now—this moment—will impact what our future becomes, why not focus on appreciating what we have now instead of focusing on what we used to have or what we might have one day? Then we're actually living fully and have no illusion about what is, was, or will be.

Considerable #2

BE CIVIL

So it's 10 pm on a Saturday night, and I'm in NYC, having a drink at a bar. Restaurant row. Mid-town. Pretty classy place. The owner is an ex-Marine turned actor and restaurateur. A good guy. Joe. Old school Italian American. Late sixties. Respectful. Non-threatening. I'm chatting with him at the bar, and about thirty feet away at the other end of the bar is an apparently inebriated gentleman who is screaming loudly about nothing in particular and carrying on in such a way that is limiting the ability of everybody else in the whole bar to hear themselves talk. In fact, it's so shrill and disturbing that everybody in the bar who knows Joe is the owner is now staring at him and appealing for him to do something.

Joe walks over to the end of the bar and politely says to the screaming man, "Sir, can you please keep it down?"

Immediately, the man screams back, "Leave me the fuck alone! Just because I'm gay doesn't give you the right to treat me that way!"

Joe, who'd had no idea about the man's sexuality and objects only to his being disruptive in this public forum, then gently reaches over to escort him out, "Sir, please."

The man pulls away from him and starts trying to hit Joe, screaming *"Don't fucking touch me!* You can't tell me what to do!"

Fortunately, at this point, two of the busboys run over and quickly escort the angry man out of the bar.

Now, there's no question members of the LGBTQ+ community have been treated poorly by far too many for far too long, but this situation had *nothing* to do with this man's sexuality. If he was being asked to leave because of his sexuality, he would have had every right to protest. But he was only being asked to please lower his voice, and then, when he refused to do that, to leave—solely because he was acting like a jerk and causing a public disturbance. Joe, the owner, never insulted him nor said anything about his sexuality—or any other aspect of his life. He politely asked him to leave because the man was behaving inappropriately and ruining the evening for all of the other patrons. And he was verbally and physically assaulted for doing so. Joe had treated the screaming man with respect, yet in return, he was treated with false accusations instead of basic civility. If the man had simply apologized and/or lowered his voice, the issue would have been easily resolved without further interruption. Instead, because the man refused to be civil at the most basic level, it was an increasingly uncomfortable experience for Joe, as well as for me and all of the other customers, who simply wanted to have a pleasant evening.

Or think of it this way: If the roles were reversed—and Joe was acting in the same uncivil manner, the other guy walked up to him and asked him to leave, and Joe responded with profanities screaming that as an Italian American he has fucking rights, etc.—the resulting lesson would still be the same. We are all members of different tribes, and we all have rights. That in itself is not the point. The point is simply that we all need to treat each other with civility, regardless of our tribe(s), and respect the rights of others.

Tomas Spath and Cassandra Dahnke, Founders of the Institute for Civility in Government, defined it this way: "Civility is claiming and caring for one's identity, needs, and beliefs without degrading someone else's in the process."

Isn't it worth thinking and talking about civility again? It's a word and concept that you don't hear about much anymore, but maybe it's time to bring it back into the vernacular. After witnessing this bar scuffle in Manhattan, it made me think about the importance of civility in our lives. Especially when you live in or visit a big city filled with lots of people, all with differences of opinion, the need for civility in order to coexist becomes apparent. A lack of civility will only lead to more division, less peaceful engagement, less happiness for us all. Perhaps, then, it's a good time to experiment with being more civil and seeing how that makes all of our lives better.

Considerable #3

KINDNESS STARTS AT THE BOTTOM

On her deathbed, my friend's mother's last words were, "Kindness starts at the bottom."

It seemed like such a profound statement, particularly given the circumstances in which she conveyed that message. "Kindness starts at the bottom."

At first, when he told me, I wasn't sure what to make of this phrase. What does it mean? What's the bottom? Why would she choose to say this before she passed?

I spent a good deal of time pondering it with him and trying to determine her meaning. In essence, I like to think of it this way: The bottom is where the foundation is laid which can enable and support every other layer or aspect of our lives. It's the most basic, fundamental aspect where it all begins. Once reduced to our core essence, we can see it is kindness that really matters, and it starts at the bottom. If kindness is the baseline for our behaviors and choices, we can then build/strengthen it and use it to lift ourselves and others.

So many of our actions in life can be transactional. I help you with something, and you reciprocate. But, as you'll read in the "Be Kind" chapter, I believe true kindness should not be transactional. It should be authentic and come from our core. My friend's mother's life was based upon two precepts—service and spirituality. She was a rabbi's wife who felt that true religion sometimes happens outside of the temple or church. I'm thankful for the perspective she shared after her life of benevolence without expectation of return. Kindness is something we can all choose to implement in our lives. It does good and feels good. And it starts at the bottom, the strongest place from which we can lift up the world.

So next time you feel low, or at the bottom, start with kindness—to yourself and then consider extending it to others. *(Please note: kindness is so important that three considerables/chapters focus on different elements of it.)*

Let's start with a fairly recent illustration of true kindness, the example of the Newfoundland townsfolk depicted in the hit musical *Come from Away*. If you aren't familiar with this story, it was based on events that took place starting on 9/11, when many planes were diverted and forced to set down at the Gander International Airport in Newfoundland, Canada. Folks from neighboring towns, including bus drivers who were on strike, set aside any differences and came together, working long hours to coordinate collection and distribution of food, blankets, diapers, shelter, etc. to the approximately 7,000 unanticipated visitors (who had arrived in a town of about 10,000 people). The Newfoundlanders offered their time, items, and kindness for several days while the planes were grounded. It was especially kind that, particularly at a time of deep mistrust and fear, they united to ensure that the thousands of people stranded in their town were comfortable and treated well. In the end, for all the people in Gander and all those on those stranded planes in Newfoundland, kindness started at the bottom on one of the worst days and, for many, it changed their life.

Considerable #4

PUTTING OTHERS DOWN
DOESN'T BUILD YOU UP

Unfortunately, the situation I described earlier in Joe's restaurant isn't unusual. Sometimes we take out our insecurities, anger, and anxiety on others in an attempt to ease our own discomfort. It can be a lot easier to be negative than to be positive. Let me explain with, well, a little anecdote from my life.

When I was a child and we'd go to visit someone, in the car on the way home we'd engage in what I would now call a full-blown social critique. For example, somebody would start with, "Did you see so and so? I think he gained a lot of weight."

Then I'd add, "Can you believe what he said about the president?"

And then somebody else would chime in, "Oh my God! Did you see those shoes that Whatshisface was wearing? And can you believe they all like that new painting they have up on the wall?"

"And did you taste those biscuits? They were hard as a rock. How can they eat that horrible food?"

This was standard operating procedure in our family, and I always assumed it was also standard driving home conversation for every family. But over the years I realized it wasn't and maybe it wasn't healthy either. I think at some level we thought it would make us feel better about ourselves, but in the end, it always made me feel worse to put down others, and as I got older, I had to relearn some habits and attitudes.

I've since made a conscious effort to be less critical, and it's not easy sometimes, but I think I am (and my relationships are) better off for it. Being less judgmental helps maintain connection rather than causing alienation. You refrain from overfocusing on what's negative or what you don't like. That means you're better able to focus on retaining your bond, which not only makes people happier but may also stave off mental, emotional, and physical issues that can arise when we feel disconnected.

After all, we all judge (perhaps it's a primal instinct, given that—especially way back when—we needed to be fully and constantly aware of our surroundings to survive), but it's what we do with the judgement and whether we give it any credibility that makes the difference. It can be worthwhile to compare oneself to others in order to learn about our differences and what we all value, but we also could stand to be kinder and more generous in our view of others, especially if they are or approach life in a way that is different than us. Sure, if the way they act is harming us we may spend energy putting people down to lift ourselves, but what we are actually doing is diminishing who we are and upending our ability to authentically connect with others.

There's a great story I heard about Mayim Bialik (she played the character Amy Farrah Fowler on the set of *Big Bang* Theory and also hosts *Jeopardy*). Whenever she was having lunch or sitting around with cast members who were gossiping about other cast members, she would politely excuse herself. Finally, one of the cast members asked her why she always did that. She answered that as an Orthodox Jew, she is forbidden to gossip about others, so she prefers to remove herself from the situation. I love that story. She did not judge her colleagues, who were acting in ways that made it seem they were better than others. She merely chose to be civil and protected herself from engaging in an act she'd prefer to avoid.

What if we all refrained from nasty gossip and putting others down, especially when we don't know another's experiences and interior landscape? Sure, gossip is fun and easy to do, and it helps connect us with others, but at what cost? Does it really make you feel better about yourself to put someone down, or are you just relieved you're not the one who is being ostracized or negated? Instead, what if you change the subject or remove yourself from conversations when others talk ill of friends? What if you pause just long enough to consider how you would feel if you were the one being gossiped about, whether or not the gossip is even based in reality? What would it be like if next time you're in a situation like that, you instead defend or lift up the person being gossiped about (who is most likely not present and can't offer any self-defense) instead? Now there's a way to feel better, rather than worse, about yourself—using the power of your voice to be kind instead of cruel.

Considerable #5

DON'T LIVE IN THE SOMEDAY AISLE

Many of us have a tendency to think about our lives in terms of the future, as in, "Someday I'll do that" or "Someday I'll travel there." This is what I call living in the "someday aisle" (right next to the canned soup aisle and in front of the produce section). Yes, it's an easy place to get lost in, but it's also important that we don't stay there too long. And its urgently important that we don't settle there. After all, life goes by quickly. As a quote attributed to Benjamin Franklin states, "You may delay, but time will not."

We all know a person and/or story like this one: I had a math teacher in high school who seemed miserable. She chain-smoked, was overweight, and was clearly unhappy. I don't know if she had a particular dream for her life, but it was clear to all in her classroom that her ideal was not being a math teacher for thirty-five years. She was simply counting the days until her much-deserved and yearned-for retirement. And then, well, within the first year of her retirement, she was greeted with a diagnosis of terminal cancer and passed away.

The tragedy of this kind of story is apparent, but now I'm asking you to look a bit more deeply. I would argue the true tragedy is that she had been living in the someday aisle for over three decades! If she had enjoyed her time as a teacher more and had done all that she could to take advantage of what she had when she had it, or if, while still teaching, she had discovered another path or hobby that she found fulfilling, I would argue that her death would still be misfortunate but not the tragedy that it was in her case.

Though we can't always determine or control our circumstances, we can choose how we approach and respond to all aspects of our lives. The choice is yours. Right now, you can consciously take yourself out of the someday aisle and put yourself into a here, now, today place.

Think about it. Have you ever put something off and then lost out because you missed the boat? It's easy to do, but if you choose to be here now, be present in this moment, and don't put off until someday what you can be doing—or at least beginning—today, you might find that more good things start coming to you.

Considerable #6

FOCUS ON WHAT YOU CAN CONTROL

One of my favorite books on writing is *Bird by Bird* by Anne LaMott. The title comes from a pivotal story in the book in which a young Annie is so overwhelmed by an assignment where she has to categorize a wide array of birds that she gives up. Thinking about all of the work she must do is so overwhelming she can't face it. When she conveys her frustration to her dad, he turns to her and says something like, "Don't worry, kid, let's just go bird by bird."

I recently moved across the country and was faced with a similar predicament. I had accumulated twenty years of stuff in my house, and the idea of getting it all removed before the new owners were going to move in seemed, well, impossible. I literally fell onto my sofa and was ready to give up. It was just too much. Fortunately, a friend suggested, "Well, for today, how about we just clean this bathroom and start there now?"

Of course, she was right. You can't clean the whole house at once. You need to go room by room, and one room (or bird, or step) at a time is much more easily do-able. Focusing on what you can control— and only what you can control—can make all the difference! Even with the ideas in this book, you can't do them all and expect everything to change for the better all at once with a snap of your fingers. If you just make a choice based on what you can do/control in this moment, you begin the journey to what's possible.

Sure, many of us are worriers. But in the end, if you are worrying about what you can't control, then you are unnecessarily getting worked up over things that are, well, beyond your control. Next time you want or need to do something and get overwhelmed or feel that some aspect of the situation is beyond your control, take a moment to stop and think, *Is this something (or is there some aspect of this) that I have the power to change?* If so, take one step, do one thing you have the power to do, which then enables you to get to the next thing that *is* in your power to do. If it's out of your control, stop worrying. There's nothing you can do about it anyway, and worrying won't get you where you need to go any faster. In fact, it will likely do the opposite, as it drains you of the energy you need to get things done and figure out your focus.

It might sound like this is just that simple, and well, it is. And unlike some of the other ideas in this book, it's quite easy too! For me, that meant getting up from the couch and allotting a segment of time to simply start packing. Then, before I knew it, I'd made enough of a dent that I could see the possibility of finishing. Ultimately, the new owners moved into the cleaned-out house, and I transported my belongings to my new home where I am now happily ensconced.

When you find yourself in a predicament in which you might not be able to choose an outcome, remember that you *can* choose your approach and response—which then shapes your circumstances. Put your focus on what you can change, and then who knows what's possible? Go from worrier to warrior(ess).

Considerable #7

LISTEN MORE, TALK LESS

This one is pretty straightforward. As you may have heard in some form, we have two ears and one mouth so we can spend more time listening than we do talking. Yet, when was the last time you felt truly listened to? How did it make you feel?

So often when we are *listening*, we are actually *thinking* about what we want to say next. Yes, the majority of us like to talk. And some of us like to talk a lot. After all, it's the way we share information and ideas and communicate with others. But all too often we don't really listen to each other, which means we stay stuck in our own stories and lose opportunities for deepening respect, understanding, and connection. A quote by Gene Knudsen Hoffman, Founder of Compassionate Listening, asserts, "An enemy is one whose story we have not heard."

It's a good idea to make a conscious effort to listen more and talk less. I have no doubt you will be glad you did. Enough said.

Considerable #8

DON'T ROOT FOR LAUNDRY

In one of his stand-up routines, comedian Jerry Seinfeld talks about the fact that when we are loyal to a sports team—when we root for the same team year after year—we are, in essence, just rooting for a specific sports jersey. He goes on to mention that when an athlete is on your favorite team, you love them, but if they get traded and are on a different team next year, you tend to dislike them and root against them. Even though it's the same person, they're now wearing different clothes, and the same fans who adored them now boo them. So isn't all sports loyalty, in the end, just rooting for laundry?

I always loved that bit. And I think its remarkably wise. Think about it. I'll use myself as an example. I was raised as a New York Giants fan from the moment I was born. My dad inculcated me with the belief that the Giants were the only team to root for. So, from birth, if I wanted to keep from being kicked out of the house, I had no choice. Every Sunday, I cheered for the Giants to win. And when they had a bad season, I had to remain a loyal fan and keep the faith. And most of the time, the Giants were pretty awful.

For many years, the whole family reluctantly repeated the refrain, "Next year, we'll be better. Next year, we're going to the Super Bowl." And then, remarkably, a few times over the past fifty years, they did go to the Super Bowl. But predictably, most years they did not. What I realized when considering Seinfeld's routine is that whether the Giants won or lost, what I actually enjoyed was the time spent with family and/or friends. Once in a while, I still watch the games, but these days I'm less connected to whether they win or lose, so I guess you can say I've stopped rooting for big blue jerseys.

This is simply a long way of saying that it's all just a construct, but it is a shared construct. So, then, talking with a stranger about a sports team can be either a way to connect to others or a divisive factor. The comedian Jim Carrey spoke about this shared construct idea when asked about being Canadian. He answered that yes, he was born in Canada, but isn't it all really just a pseudo-construct? Didn't some guys one day just draw some lines and then everybody all agreed: *Okay, you all on that side of the line are Americans and us all on this side of the line, we're now Canadians*? And doesn't the same thing apply to the American states? *You are standing over there in Rhode Island and I'm standing over here in Connecticut, and let's agree those are pretty darn good names for these particular tracts of land here, and so now we're good, right?*

Seinfeld and Carrey, like all good comedians, are on to something. They're looking at what we all experience, hold onto with intense passion, and even take for granted every day, but seeing humor in it and drawing our attention to it in a way that makes us reflect a little more deeply on life and the ways we think and act. This idea of it all just being a construct based upon societal trust in someone's original idea goes beyond observations of stand-up comedians. It is everywhere in our culture.

Take the gold standard behind US currency. At one time, you could take a dollar bill to the US Treasury and say, "I demand you give me one dollar in gold for this bill." This was the gold standard, and it was originally used to give our currency validity. For me, as a merchant, to accept a green piece of paper and, in return, give you something of real value like a ham sandwich, I needed to believe that the green piece of paper represented something tangible and of value: *gold!*

However, on June 5, 1933, the US government removed the gold standard, and suddenly, the only thing backing the dollar bill was our faith in the legitimacy of US legal tender and the US Treasury who issued it. We are seeing a similar situation now with the rise of cryptocurrencies. As long as enough people buy into the legitimacy of crypto as a form of currency, it will have value, but if the government outlaws it and people refuse to honor it, it could suddenly go *poof* and lose all its value.

Mutually agreed upon faith and trust – that's what it's all about, folks.

On a final note here, some of these constructs are actually codified as laws, but even laws as constructs can change. Women weren't allowed to vote in the nineteenth century, and then the law changed in 1920, and they suddenly became voters. *Boom!*

No matter how you look at it, whether you are talking sports team jerseys, national boundaries, voting rights, or the gold standard, it's all just a function of agreed-upon constructs that dictate who we are and how we are to act with each other. If you agree to be part of society, you inherently also agree to go along with society's constructs. With that in mind, go ahead and root for or against the New York Giants this season, but also remember that at a core level you are simply rooting for or against some blue and red laundry.

Considerable #9

IT'S OKAY TO BE SAD FOR A WHILE

We live in a society that prioritizes happiness. At the same time, the CDC has recently stated there's a loneliness epidemic in the country, and the United Kingdom has appointed a Minister for Loneliness. Additionally, as of this writing, the Anxiety and Depression Association of America reports on its website (https://adaa.org) that over 40 million Americans suffer from anxiety disorders each year and over 250 million people around the world live with depression.

Many of us feel compelled to always put on a happy face, often despite actually feeling sad. But the problem isn't trying to be happy; it's ignoring or not honoring sadness when that's what's present. You can't change what you pretend doesn't exist and aren't willing to be aware of and examine. And it's only when one sits with one's sadness (and other emotions, but for the sake of this chapter I'm sticking with sadness, since that's a common feeling which is often undermined or dismissed) that one can then move through it and eventually return to feeling better.

(Please note: When I speak of sadness, it's not about someone who is experiencing all-pervasive sadness or depression, especially if it's been ongoing,

which I don't want to ignore or minimize. In that case, it may be advisable to consult a medical professional such as a physician or therapist.)

My favorite book that deals with this issue is the wonderful little epistolary novel, Rilke's *Letters to a Young Poet*. In this classic text, the poet, Rainer Marie Rilke, who dealt with depression all his life, wrote a series of letters to an aspiring and struggling young poet. Over the course of their interaction, what one begins to see is that this is more than a book for aspiring poets. This is a book for any human being who struggles with the difficulties of being alive. This is a book about what it takes to find meaning in one's life. And it could only have been written by someone who struggled deeply with the most difficult questions of life.

As a poet, Rilke dedicated his life to such questions, and the answers he provides in these letters are profound. My favorite is a letter in which he speaks of the necessity of depression and sadness. He argues that it is only a result of experiencing true sadness and sitting with it and living it, and then—and only then—passing through it to the other side that we can one day find true happiness and meaning in our lives. Rilke urges his young poet, therefore, not to avoid sadness but to embrace it in order to live through it and get to the other side of it knowing it won't last forever. That, then, becomes his answer and his solution and his best advice.

There is a saying, "That which we resist, persists." Instead of ignoring or denying feelings that make you uncomfortable, it can be life-changing to explore your sadness (and other emotions). Only then can it be transformed so you don't stay stuck or get surprised when it returns, perhaps even more vehemently. It doesn't have to be time-consuming (again, simple though not always easy). For example, you might feel some release after a good cry or writing it out, talking with someone you trust, or even considering what's behind the sadness while running or working out at the gym. The ways to address emotions are numerous.

Though I couldn't change the situation when my dad died and the sadness didn't go away quickly (and still happens, though less frequently as the years pass), writing about him—and letting the tears flow if they came—freed up enough energy that I could breathe again. Then, the sadness dissipated enough so I didn't feel as overwhelmed and could function without feeling so weighted down. If we tend to the weeds to clear the space, we have more room for new life to flourish.

In the end, they say grief comes in waves. So when the sadness hits, don't fight it. Don't ignore it. Don't reject it. Ride the wave and trust that it will take you to a better place.

Considerable #10

CHOOSE TO CELEBRATE

Though it's key to acknowledge, allow, and integrate your sadness—understanding it's part of you and needs to be "heard" if you're to be whole— it's just as vital to celebrate your life.

Hopefully when you feel sad it will only be for a brief period, and in life's inevitable ebb and flow, you'll have the ability to move beyond that sadness (which may include the help of prescribed medication, exercise, stress reduction practices, etc.). That's what I want to talk about here—eventually moving beyond the sadness and giving time and weight to celebrating life in small and large ways. Let me explain.

I remember being pretty despondent after a play I had worked on for years and felt proud of was trounced on by the critics and bombed—on opening night. Nearly a decade of hard work, and, in one night it was all over. The play closed, and for weeks I grappled with feeling as if I'd never be able to write again and nobody would ever hire me again. Before it had barely begun, my playwriting career would be over. What would I do then? It was not a good time in my life. Since we can't always get through the sad times alone, I reached out to a writer friend of mine who gave me some great advice.

He asked me what my favorite restaurant was.

I told him but then asked, a bit irritated that he was seeming to ignore my current plight, "What the hell does that have to do with anything?"

He answered by telling me to go there and treat myself to a wonderful meal and celebrate my life.

I was stunned. Was he even listening to what I was saying? How could I celebrate my life? I had just been murdered by the critics. My play had closed. I was a failure. Everything I had worked for was torn to pieces in no time at all. What was there to celebrate?

He smiled and repeated his suggestion to go out. Eat. Enjoy a festive meal. Try to laugh a little. Treat yourself. What you'll find is that you'll soon be feeling better, which offers some perspective so you can see that things really are—and will be—okay. Life will go on. The sun will rise again tomorrow.

And you know what? Though I still felt sad, I took his advice, which turned out to be quite sage. Life will keep moving forward, and I can find aspects to still celebrate.

You are how you feel, so even when you go through a rough patch (and after you're through it), remember to honor your life by celebrating some aspect of it. You'll gain some clarity and perspective and see that it's not the end of the world. There will be other highs and lows. You're not six feet under. You can simmer in sadness and look for things that keep you mired there by proving and deepening the awful feeling, or you can look for things to celebrate. Once again, though choice may be limited—my choice would have been that the play was a major success, after all—you can still choose how you perceive the situation and how you'll respond to/approach it from this point forward.

You can be upset when things don't work out. You can also still choose to celebrate. Make a big deal about that walk you just took (and how you're taking care of your health) and that bird you just heard singing (and how amazing that nature has such diversity and beauty). Breathe in fresh air and exhale. Delight in how that luscious hot dog you had for lunch today still makes your mouth water at the memory. Realize how lucky you are to be alive. Celebrate! Honor your life, and you're likely to enjoy the resulting feeling so much that you will make it a more frequent healthy habit.

You are what you feel! Celebrate you and what you treasure about yourself and your life. When you acknowledge and savor the stuff you enjoy, not only does it remind you of life's pleasures, but it can also help build resilience to deal with the inevitable stresses that will arise.

Considerable #11

BE GRATEFUL AND APPRECIATIVE

This one is a further expression of celebration and how you can deepen its impact. Let me explain with another anecdote.

Before my wedding day, a friend told me that it will go by really fast and suggested that on the big day—when everybody is celebrating, laughing, dancing, and having a good time—stop and look around and really appreciate it before it all disappears. And I took their advice to heart. Several times over the course of the day. Really stopping for a moment and taking it all in. Savoring it. Looking around at my family and friends and creating a special memory, thankful to be having that experience together. I was so grateful that I did, because it was over so quickly and what remained from the day were those memories and the feelings of gratitude for all it represented.

I think this applies to so much more than just wedding days. On a daily basis, while you are spending time on your own or hanging out with friends or family, take a moment to acknowledge something you are thankful for. One thing that makes life great in this moment, something you can appreciate. This is it. Right here. Right now. This is the best of the best. A beautiful moment. This is your life, formed one moment at a time. Simply acknowledge and enjoy it. Appreciate it. Breathe it in. And then breathe it out. Articulate your feelings about how special it all is. Allow yourself to acknowledge how fortunate you are that you get to have this experience. Notice if your experience matches scientific study results showing how gratitude can enhance relationships, help diminish stress, and just make you feel better and more optimistic about the world, yourself, and others.

And then lather, rinse, repeat. After all, like building and maintaining any muscle, we need to exercise appreciation and gratitude frequently or occasionally, not just once).

Considerable #12

DON'T COMPARE, DON'T COMPETE

It's natural to compare oneself to others and, in life's yin and yang, there may be occasions where it even feels somewhat motivating. Don't do it. Why? There is only one you. Your path is your own. Comparing your journey to that of anyone else's is simply unrealistic and may even inevitably result in some disappointment or frustration as well as wasted time and energy.

I came to learn this truth when I took a playwriting course during my senior year at Yale. It changed my life. I fell in love with playwriting and found that I could stay up all night writing, and the words just poured out of me. I had found my life's calling.

Now, there was this one other guy in my class who was also a prolific writer. We both applied to UCLA Film School's screenwriting program and were both accepted. They took only twelve people a year, so it was a great honor. We both graduated college and moved to Los Angeles. Soon, we were taking grad courses on screenwriting together and learning our craft. However, unlike me, he had acquired an agent and within a few months was hired to be a staff writer on the renowned TV series *Cheers*.

He dropped out of grad school and joined the *Cheer*s writing room as a full-time staff writer. At that time, *Cheer*s was the number one sitcom in the nation, and this was when people still watched network TV on a TV, so it was a *very big deal*. Essentially, he had gone from just starting out to the pinnacle of success in the world of writing literally overnight, or at least that's what it seemed like to me.

And then, in an act of thoughtfulness—which I, at the time, saw as showing off—he invited me to a taping of an episode that he had penned. Of course I went, and I will never forget looking down at the sound stage and seeing him there in a director's chair, looking over at the actors mouthing his words and then over at me and smiling.

Boy, was I ever jealous! It tore at my heart! You see, I had made our friendship into a competition. We had both started out from the same place and been on a similar journey, but boy oh boy, did he get to the finish line a lot faster than me. I wanted to get there but wasn't 100 percent sure I would, whereas he had already reached a high level of Hollywood success. In response, I was insecure and angry and wished for his failure, which left me feeling shitty about myself. For the next two years, he was working on the show while I was struggling, and I beat myself up about it. A lot. And then, as the years passed, we lost touch, and our friendship dissolved.

What did my approach to all this accomplish? Not much of anything other than a lot of hours spent feeling upset about my pace up the ladder of success and resentful of his. It didn't inspire me to greatness, and it didn't make me a better writer (or person, for that matter), and there were really no lessons to be learned except, well, this one. Life is not a competition, and beating yourself up only leaves you bruised and battered. Oh sure, there are forums where temporary competition is central, such as in sports. And that sense can inspire some to play better or work harder. But it doesn't work that way in life.

We all have a unique path (after all, since there is only one you, no one else can offer what you bring into the world), and we may wish it would be as straight and short as possible, but that ain't usually what happens. Embrace the bumpy and windy road that is your unique adventure. If you do, rather than wasting time comparing yourself to others, you'll be happier (and healthier and have more authentic relationships).

Comparing yourself to others only makes you feel bad about yourself and/or others and wastes the time you could be using to make your life better. What's the good in that? In the end, if you want to compete, do it with yourself so you keep enhancing and improving your life.

Considerable #13

EVEN THE GOAT DIDN'T BAT OVER .500

Many people believe that Ted Williams was the greatest hitter ever to play baseball. Some call him the GOAT (greatest of all time). His best season batting average of .407 was and remains the highest batting average of any baseball player in the modern history of the game. Just for perspective: a batting average of .407 means that four out of ten times when he came up to bat, he got a hit.

In other words, the greatest hitter in the history of baseball still didn't get a hit more than half the time.

Let that sink in. More than 50 percent of the time, the world's greatest hitter still struck out or failed to hit the ball safely to get on base.

What that should mean to us all is simply this – be kinder to, and have more patience with, yourself. We all fail. A lot. And that's okay. It helps us learn and get better. In fact, even more than what happens, it's how we respond to it that can make the difference in what our life will be like moving forward.

Even people who are doing what they love for a living can spend a good percentage of time not liking aspects of what they are doing. I love to write, paint, golf, and play tennis, but that doesn't mean I don't get frustrated by losing in sports and not selling my artistic work. So even after achieving a modicum of success in your chosen field, the failures keep coming and you'll keep needing to go back to bat with your head held high.

You will never have a 100 percent perfect batting average in whatever field of endeavor you choose. There's a good deal in life that is not going to be wonderful. How might your life change if you celebrate your successes (and what it took to achieve them) while also learning from the failures or incompletions along the way, seeing all of it as part of the whole process of being alive? After all, if you can be successful in four out of ten of your attempts, then you're doing as well as the greatest hitter of all time.

Considerable #14

STOP WAITING FOR PEOPLE TO ACKNOWLEDGE/APPRECIATE YOU

I've come to learn it's best to do good simply for the sake of doing good. Stop waiting for people to acknowledge and appreciate you. Does your dog say thank you when you give it food? No. We all can become self-absorbed at times. We need to get over ourselves. If you do something well-meaning, do it for the sake of doing it. Instead of expending energy on expecting a particular response, revel in how gratifying it is to be considerate of others. Acknowledge yourself and forget feeling the need to get something in return from anyone else, including any kudos or thanks. If your intent is genuine, thanks don't matter, and then if you are acknowledged, let it be the icing on an already-delicious cake.

I went to college with a guy who ended up making a lot of money in the energy business. He could do anything he wants with it, but one thing he chooses to do every December is hang out in a large discount box store with a pocket filled with fifty $100 bills. He tries to be inconspicuous while wandering the aisles looking for people who might not be able to afford holiday presents for their loved ones. He says that he can always tell when somebody really needs the money. He hangs back and tries to blend in at the store and looks for those who seem most in need of help.

And when he quietly approaches them and presents them with his little green $100 gift, he can see that need turn to joy before he walks away to find the next recipient. He's not doing it for the kudos. He doesn't tell them his name or stick around to be praised. He merely takes pleasure in giving and gets a tremendous rush from seeing how he can change lives and bring happiness to others with one simple gesture.

Of course, you don't need money to do good. You can volunteer; help someone in need; call on an older person who lives alone; leave a sweet note for a friend, lover, delivery person; offer to babysit; place positive reviews on a blog; etc.

And who knows how one kind gesture can change someone's life? The actress and comedienne Carol Burnett has been known to share her personal story about doing an opera workshop in college. Her professor invited the students to a black-tie party in San Diego to provide the entertainment, after which he'd grade them on their performance. She did a scene from *Annie Get Your Gun*, after which she was stealing hors d'oeuvres in a napkin to take home to her grandmother (whose rent at that time was in the vicinity of $30/month), when she felt a tap on her shoulder. She turned to see a man in a tuxedo and his wife in a fancy dress. He asked what she wanted to do with her life. When she mentioned acting in New York, he asked why she wasn't already there, to which she responded that she didn't have the means. He offered to lend her the money, as he believed in her talent, and wrote a $1,000 check, which enabled her to go to New York. His only stipulations were that she pay it back in five years (no interest), she use the money to go to New York and act, she never reveal his name, and if she did well, she'd help others out. Years later, after she launched her own television show, the man and his wife invited her to lunch, after which the wife told her that whenever Burnett's name came up when they were with friends, the man never said a word. Evidently, someone had helped him achieve success and he was simply paying it forward. Giving, at its best, changes lives and begets more giving.

I'm sure you can think of lots of creative ways to give or give back (including being the kind of person who offers thanks to others). Try one or two of them, knowing from the start that having the genuine intent to be kind is enough and that you don't need any response. See how it makes you feel.

Considerable #15

LEAVE THE JUDGING TO OTHERS

I'll never forget attending a little impromptu dance when I was in college. I was in New Hampshire campaigning for a presidential candidate who shall remain nameless. A bunch of us college students from schools all over New England were there, though I didn't know anybody from outside of our school. We worked hard all weekend trying to win a few coveted votes from those wacky but lovable New Hampshire residents.

In general, it felt like we had pretty much failed and hardly made a dent in the political consciousness of the local voters. But we had fought the good fight, and the campaign thought that we deserved a few cases of beer and a little sock-hop. So the good people running the campaign pushed aside all the furniture, turned on a boom box (after all, this was still the 1980s), and we had ourselves a little social!

There I was with my buddy from college by my side, watching everybody else dancing. Just two geeky college kids trying not to feel like outsiders. We looked at the people on the dance floor and knew they were bright and educated college students, but they were not exactly a group of talented dancers.

However, the music was pretty good, the beer was decent, and they were letting loose and simply having fun. And you know what? Most of them didn't care about the quality of their dance moves. They were just enjoying themselves and dancing together.

But I couldn't help myself. I turned to my friend and rolled my eyes.

He looked back at me and said, "What's wrong? Go. Dance. Have fun."

"I can't. I'm not a good dancer. I'll look stupid."

He laughed and then said, "Do you think anybody here is a good dancer?"

"Clearly not."

"So what are you worried about? Have fun. Dance. Enjoy yourself."

But I couldn't do it. I was too caught up in the way I would look. It was silly, I know. But hey, I was young and vain and worried about how I might appear in the eyes of the others. And mind you, this was before smartphones with cameras and social media, so there was no way anybody who wasn't at this event would ever even see how poorly I danced. Yet, I still refused to trip the light fantastic.

In retrospect, I still look back on that night and think how sad it is that I acted that way. I was too busy judging others and myself to just go out there and have a good time. I missed an opportunity to enjoy myself and the people I was there with. Instead, I spent the time literally making myself miserable. That was a mistake, and I hope that today I might act a little bit differently.

What's the oft-repeated advice about living your life with joyful abandon in a way that's true to you? I think it goes something like this: "Dance like nobody's watching." Because the truth is, we spend lots of time being self-conscious despite the probability that no one is watching. Most people really don't care about how you dance. They are too concerned with themselves and how they look out there. And even on the off chance they do, that tells you more about them than you, so leave them to their sideline judgements while you just have fun living. If it looks fun and you want to dance, then go dance.

In the end, try not to judge yourself and others as much. The more focus you put on judgement, the less time you just enjoy living. It's hard, but if you succeed in doing it, you are likely to spend less time feeling the negativity that comes with judging and more time finding things to appreciate. No doubt, that alone will add to your happiness.

Considerable #16

LIFE IS NOT A SAFE SPACE

I understand the need for safe spaces where we can breathe and gain some perspective, especially as we try to co-exist in this seemingly divided and hostile moment. And I get the human desire to try to create safe spaces to minimize hurt. But the very nature of life is such that it's not a safe space. No one avoids all pain or lives forever. We all experience heartache and hardship. We all eventually die. The world is filled with viruses and fires and tornadoes and cancer and breakups and the like. Trying to convince ourselves otherwise or thinking we can avoid every painful possibility, is folly.

This became doubly clear to me when Covid first struck. My next-door neighbor is a wise man and a practicing therapist. He is also Armenian, and he and his family are survivors of the Armenian genocide. When Covid arrived and the world seem to be spinning out of control, I asked him what he thought of everything that was going on. He always speaks in a calm voice, and he told me that, for him, nothing had really changed. He sees clients eight hours a day four days a week. He does not believe in Zoom, and he does what he can for the people who come to see him.

I was kind of stunned, so I asked, "Wait, hasn't Covid changed all that?"

He smiled and answered, "Look, I believe that the majority of Americans have been living in a sort of Disneyland for their entire lives so that the irregularities in their lives now must come as a real shock to them. But for me, I always knew life here as a sort of Disneyland. It's a bit unreal, and as a result, none of these irregularities have much effect on me. You see, when your starting point is a world filled with hatred and genocide, everything else pales in comparison. And as a result, it's easier for me than a lot of Americans not to get bent out of shape over changes in our so-called society. Sure, I wear a mask and take precautions, but I still meet my clients in person and refuse to do Zoom tele-conferencing."

Considering his perspective made me realize that without the illusion of the security of a safe space, we are better able to handle the inevitable ups and downs of life. Yes?

Considerable #17

SOMETIMES THINGS DON'T HAPPEN
FOR A REASON

It's comforting to think that everything happens for a reason, and perhaps many things do happen for a reason. But when a child gets a terminal illness or a young parent dies suddenly, it's hard to see a reason for such a tragedy. In those kinds of situations, the idea that everything always happens for a reason doesn't seem to hold true and just sounds cliché. I think a better precept is simply this: Sometimes things happen for a reason and, well, sometimes they don't. And that's okay either way. Life is a dynamic process.

We human beings want to make sense of the seemingly arbitrary and random events that occur in our lives. It feels too overwhelming to think there is no reason. Justifying events by saying everything happens for a reason makes sense in this context, as it helps us feel better about the events in our lives.

If you see a reason behind a series of events in your life and it helps things make sense, fantastic! Create meaning for yourself. But if you don't, that's okay too. Everything doesn't have to happen for a reason. The burden of trying to make sense of negative events, especially as they are happening, can be a bit overwhelming and can use up the internal resources needed to cope with the event itself.

On the other hand, maybe you will be able to see a reason for it one day and you will learn from it. Either way, you know what? It's all part of the experience of being alive. Embrace it.

Considerable #18

DEATH IS SCARY, BUT IT'S BEST
TO TALK ABOUT IT

This musing comes from a dear friend and the author of the foreword, Irwin Kula. There's so much wisdom in it that I wanted to share it as he sent it to me. As a Rabbi, he's spent a good deal of time dealing with death, so there's much to learn from his sagacity here with this difficult subject.

We don't know what to write or say in these situations because what we really want is to make things all right and we can't. Nothing reminds us of how little control over life we have than death, particularly that of a younger person. It threatens the order, stability, security we impose on the chaos and randomness and unfairness that erupts into life. In other words, we don't know what to say or write because of our fear this could happen to us and know that no words would make a difference or change the outcome.

So, first, we have to feel this fear and vulnerability and not make believe anything we say or write is going to make things alright. We have to own our own fear and our own inability to find the "right words." Then we have to focus away from ourselves and onto the person who is actually vulnerable. And each person is unique, and nothing is more unique than our own dying—though, paradoxically, it is something we all do no matter what. Knowing the person and knowing our relationship to that person, we can then decide what words to say or write—words that won't make everything right but that will, appropriate to the relationship, simply do this:

A. Let the person know you are thinking about them (as nothing is lonelier than dying).

B. Express and acknowledge your sadness at hearing the news.

C. Share something specific that you personally learned from, remember, or experienced with the person that has stayed with you or impacted you. (This is a way of saying the person is important and her memory will endure. Remember, we die twice—the first time when we physically die and the next time when there is no one who remembers us.)

D. Express your hope and blessing that, given we all wish reality would be different, you hope and pray that this last period of her life will be filled with [the] comforting love of family and friends, the knowledge that she has led a good life and impacted many people, and the wisdom to teach us all about the end of life.

If it is appropriate to the relationship and circumstances to visit, and the person would want such a visit, then I would make sure to try to arrange it.

You see, the wisdom here is: the more honest and sensitive you are to the emotion of the reality, the more comforting you will be.

By the way, here is what we know from studies: People at the end of life have three fundamental concerns and fears.

1. They don't want to be in pain.

2. They don't want to be a burden to those they love.

3. They want to know they will be remembered, that their life meant something to people!

Considerable #19

YOU'RE NOT THE CUSTODIAN OF OTHERS' EMOTIONAL WELL-BEING

We tend to wonder or worry about people's feelings. We want to take care of others and to please them. Though that's certainly not a bad thing, ultimately, we are each responsible for our own emotional well-being. You can affect how someone may feel, but you can't control/make their feelings happen or alter them. Only they can. And vice versa. While being kind to others is important, we also need to be kind to ourselves. In fact, in order to genuinely be able to be there for others, we need to start with ourselves. In other words, an empty well has nothing to offer.

If you consider and tend to others' feelings at the expense of your own, you become depleted. You are that empty well. I'm not advocating putting yourself first in all situations or being selfish, but I am advocating doing what you need to do (as long as your behaviors are not harmful) to safeguard your own emotional well-being and to fully function. When you are emotionally healthy, you are better able to both revel in life's delights and deal with life's adversity and stresses. You take responsibility for yourself rather than being divisive and wasting time by placing blame elsewhere. If someone else gets mad when you tend to your emotional well-being and follow your heart, instead of denying your feelings to stop from upsetting them, it may be important to set boundaries.

In one kind of example, let's say your parents always wanted you to go into a profession like medicine or law but you always wanted to be an artist. If they tell you that going to art school would upset them and you then give up your dreams because you don't want to disappoint them, you're attempting to take care of their feelings at the expense of yours. And the likelihood is that you will at some point regret your choice and/or end up resenting them for your choice. It's thoughtful for everyone involved to be mindful of their reactions and their impact on each other's current thinking, but the key is you own your own feelings and to respond in ways that are constructive and thoughtful, rather than divisive or accusatory.

In another example, consider how you feel if someone is bothered by something you've said or done and starts an intense conversation with "It's your fault. You made me feel ____" versus "When this happened, I felt ____" When someone says your behavior "makes" them miserable or upset or angry, the fact is that they may feel that way, and it may be a response to your behavior, but you did not create that feeling, nor are you responsible for changing it (or have the power to do so). The same goes for all of us. Again, this does not apply to a case in which there is harm done, which should be avoided.

When taking responsibility for the way you feel, if you release the need to constantly please everybody and that inadvertently causes another person some displeasure, you can certainly apologize and try to rectify the situation (taking into account everyone's opinions and feelings while knowing no one can change anyone else). You don't need to take on their upset or hold onto it. The goal is to try to stay true to yourself while simultaneously caring about and respecting others and where they may be emotionally (as long as they are also not harming you in some way).

I have come to believe in and love this quote, which has been attributed to film director Mike Nichols: "Every relationship needs a rose and a gardener." It seems so true, and I think the ideal relationship is one in which both partners take turns being both roses and gardeners at certain moments in their relationship. So, it's never exactly fifty/fifty, but there are moments that are more about you and moments that are more about them.

We can tend to each other, but we first need to be our own gardener *and* rose in order to have the energy and opportunity to thrive. Maybe the quote should be changed to, "Be both a rose and a gardener to yourself and in your relationships, and they will both flourish." I know that I tend to enjoy being a rose, but I also get great pleasure from cooking for and buying presents for the people I care about, so I find the most happiness when I can bounce back and forth between the two. We don't always get things right, so it's good to keep being mindful and self-aware and trying again. Overall, it's helpful to remember that if your family, friends, or partner don't like your behaviors, you can care for and about them without taking responsibility for their feelings. Just as they can do with you.

Yet again, none of this is easy, but all of it is worth thinking about, yes?

Considerable #20

HAVE A SIMILAR SHARED FANTASY
OF THE FUTURE

L ots of things lead to the thriving or failure of a relationship, be it a romantic, familial, or even friendship or business connection. After struggling with relationships (including a divorce) over the course of several decades and much therapy, I have come to see that one of the most important aspects of relationships is that they are based upon a usually unspoken but hopefully *mutually agreed-upon fantasy of the future.*

What do I mean by this? Well, simply put, as long as both parties in the relationship share a similar fantasy of the future, the relationship will have a more solid foundation from which to foster growth and fulfillment. It stands a better chance at resilience and harmony and longevity. Think about it. If you are dating someone who is dreaming of getting married and spending their life with you in a monogamous relationship while you are dreaming about hanging out with lots of different people in a polyamorous arrangement without the commitment of marriage, the relationship most likely ain't going to last long. Seriously, there are some situations where you can compromise and others in which two people's desires are mutually exclusive. In case of the latter, perhaps it's best you both move on. And the sooner the better so that you can find what (and who) it is you want.

As another example, consider a relationship with a work colleague. What might happen if one person sees the interaction as a transactional one based solely upon the fact that both parties work together while the other person sees it as a deep, lasting friendship that goes way beyond the confines of the workplace? Without communicating or reaching some understanding or compromise, there's likely to be frustration and/or hurt, which can also affect their ability to work together effectively.

I know that in this book I also speak of celebrating differences and being civil, and I still say all of these are important and not dissimilar, though they may be called for in different circumstances or at different times in relationship. The way I see it, being able to manage our differences and our dissimilar ideas and expectations is rooted in good communication. Without sharing our truths, division is likely to be inevitable. So, yes, as a basic foundation for connection, I want to celebrate our differences, and then from there, we need to communicate with respect and civility as the primary step to bridging these differences in order to move forward together and avert misunderstandings.

It's worth it to work on relationships and communicate about where desires converge and diverge. Though no two people are the same, if you have polar opposite ideas of what you want, that can cause difficulty, misunderstandings, and likely rifts in connection, particularly if it's an intimate relationship.

Deciding whether or not to move on from that relationship is up to you. But, if nothing else, maybe this chapter/considerable will inspire you to at least talk with a friend, colleague, or partner about who they are, including their hopes and dreams and fantasies of the future. I bet you might learn a little something about them and what they want—and perhaps more about yourself as well. Honest communication, exploring who you/they are and what you/they want in life can deepen the relationship—or, if you're not in alignment, it can clarify with more certainty that it's best to move on. In that case, letting go with grace can ease what might otherwise be an even more painful situation.

In the end, it all comes down to good communication. Often in life we want others to be mind readers, and we assume they know what we are thinking and feeling when, in reality, they don't. So it's good to speak up to ensure you make the journey together with a shared idea of where you're headed.

Considerable #21

GUILT IS A WASTED EMOTION

Many years ago, I was fortunate to be on a panel with the man who wrote one of the first and most important books on screenwriting, Syd Field. I was in awe of him, but after the panel was over, I gathered my courage and approached him and started chatting. He was quite friendly, and I discovered he was very much into meditation and Eastern religious pursuits. We spoke for a while, and though I can't remember now what the specifics were, I expressed to him how guilty I was feeling about something I had done or said.

He just stopped and looked at me and said, "Rich, guilt is a wasted emotion."

I'll never forget those words. Ever since I was a child, I've been wracked with guilt over all the mistakes I've made, and then, *boom*, with just a few words, he lifted my curse. Yes, so much of my life had been driven by guilt, and in one sentence, he was asserting I didn't have to keep living that way. And there it was—another lesson that is simple, though not easy. Even as an adult, I still carried guilt for talking back to my parents as a child or being disrespectful or bratty. His words helped me realize the difference between having a feeling versus unnecessarily holding onto it forever like an anchor, which would not change anything I'd said or done but simply be a drag and prevent me from living my life.

Even for Syd, this realization did not happen overnight. It had taken years of spiritual practice for him to learn to let go of his own version of hanging onto guilt. By sharing what he had learned, he was offering me another perspective and teaching me to do the same.

How many of us have spent much of our lives feeling guilty for things we regret doing or saying? Now, I'm not advising that your life should be guilt-free (after all, if you realize you've done something wrong and feel remorse, it shows you have a conscience). But if you choose to do something that induces guilt, rather than just getting mired in and spending a lot of time feeling lousy about yourself, you may find it helpful to use the time to examine what you're feeling and why.

In and of itself, feeling guilty changes nothing and accomplishes nothing. Instead of stewing in your guilt, you can learn from it. You can focus on what you could do differently in the future or what you can do right now to rectify the situation. And remember, though a quick glance backward can occasionally offer a helpful perspective, the longer you do it, the more likely it will only lead to tripping. Look forward. That's where you're headed.

Okay, you did something wrong. We all (and I do mean *all*) make mistakes and trip up. But we can look at our mistakes and learn from them and move forward, hopefully not repeating our error ever again.

Regardless of how you choose to handle perceived mistakes or errors in judgement, Syd taught me that just feeling guilty and beating yourself up without doing anything to rectify the situation isn't going to help anyone. We've all been on both sides of the fence, so it's good to learn to be kinder to yourself—and to others when they make inevitable missteps—and keep moving forward toward more desirable results and relationships.

Considerable #22

DON'T GIVE UNSOLICITED ADVICE-
YOU CAN'T UNFRIEND FAMILY

We tend to want to give advice to others. Resist that desire unless someone has specifically requested your input. After all, when have you enjoyed someone "shoulding" you, especially without room for or recognition of your own input or consideration?

Sure, you can argue that this chapter and book are offering advice, even if you agree it's well-meaning. But I would say this is a sharing of ideas garnered from experiences that have helped me get through some tough times and you are choosing to read it. You can turn the page at any time. I can let you know what's been helpful to me, hoping you'll find some nuggets here to make life easier for you, without your feeling you've been *should* upon.

The key issue here is solicitation. Did the other person ask for your advice? Or did you ask if they wanted to hear your perspective? If they asked for or welcomed your input, go for it. Advise away! But if they didn't, I've learned it's best to try to withhold it. Refrain. Advice is useful only if the person wants to receive it. If they don't ask for it, don't give it. And even when you do get asked and do give advice, don't be tied to their following it. Again, you're not responsible for another's well-being.

This is yet another of the considerables that may be easier said than done. But I've learned that when I have the urge to give advice to others, it's good to take a breath and simply consider, *Did they ask to hear this*? If not, I keep my mouth shut.

On the flip side, if someone offers you unsolicited advice, you can politely stop them, or you might consider hearing what they have to say. I often find myself on the receiving end of advice from someone who thinks they have something to offer or it's in my best interest to listen to their wisdom. Sure, I didn't ask for it, but who knows? Maybe there's something in what they're saying that might be of use to me. So it can be helpful to stay open to just listening without feeling compelled to follow any and all advice received.

Refraining from offering unsolicited advice can be easier for some of us to do with non-family members. But for some reason, we sometimes feel like we can say things to family members that we would never say to anyone else. I would argue that if you can't say it to a stranger or even a friend or they haven't asked for your advice, you shouldn't say it to a family member either.

With that said, I have another partial considerable which falls under the umbrella of this chapter that I want to share with you: *You can't unfriend family.* This one was created by our cultural conditioning over the millennia, and it's a truism worth considering. These days, when it's so easy to just unfriend, block, delete, ghost, and dispose of other human beings, we are all still members of some sort of family unit that cannot easily be deleted. The fact that you are stuck with family members for life, even if you do try to delete them, means that you may need to confront the issues that they raise (whether on your own or with them), and maybe awareness and growth can come from that.

Sure, at times you might want to just block and delete a family member who's giving unsolicited advice or saying something you don't want to hear, but why not reconsider? I've seen so many estranged family members, and I think, in the end, most people regret not trying harder to stay connected or at least narrowing the vast distance between each other. I've found that simply agreeing to listen to unwanted advice from a family member—while knowing you don't necessarily need to follow it and it may not feel right for you down the road—might allow you to salvage a family relationship that might otherwise have been lost.

Considerable #23

VALUE EXPERIENCES OVER OBJECTS

Here is the central paradox of the modern American economy. Since 1960, the average income of Americans has tripled, but the percentage of people who are happy has gone down, thus showing that money and happiness are not linked. We know this and pay lip service to this, but still, even though we need some money for the essentials, we spend our lives pursuing many times the amount of wealth we will truly ever need. We buy bigger houses and fancier cars and weigh ourselves down with debt. Why?

I think it's a function of how successful the consumer culture is. People like things. Marketers know this and push all the right buttons to convince us we need much more than we really do. So we also come to believe we need much more money than is necessary. Do we really need that Viking stove when a Kenmore stove will do just fine? Do we really need Rolex when an Apple watch does more?

Now enter the Millennials, the first generation in American history to have less wealth than their parents. As a result, Millennials today tend to desire minimalism and to want less, not more. In that process, they have essentially been forced to understand a truth that many other generations have not: It's not the material goods you own that matter but the experiences you have and share with others that are truly important.

Think about it. On your deathbed, will you really care about that fancy car you purchased, or will you remember that week you spent with friends on vacation—or even having family and/or friends over and just hanging out? For me, I know when I lost my dad, the memories I most treasured were of the times just spent watching *Seinfeld* together or when I helped him with his computer or served him some good soup. In retrospect, I learned that it was the smaller, quieter moments—which usually revolved around shared experiences and didn't require lots of money or things—that were the most meaningful and what I hold onto now that he's gone.

In keeping with this idea, here's another story. In the transcripts of the last conversations of people who died on 9/11—those who were on the planes that went down or in the twin towers—there is a striking similarity. For all those people, when they realized they had only a few short minutes left to live, they didn't worry about their second homes in Florida or the brand of their cars or any other item they had purchased. They all called loved ones to say, "I love you." It was the people they cherished who they considered when it came down to life and death.

If this shows us anything, perhaps it's that even if you have lots of things, it's best to prioritize and acknowledge what—and who—you truly value in life well before getting so close to death that there is no more time to appreciate or spend together. Presence is a great gift. And you don't need anything but each other to make your time together an experience to remember.

Considerable #24

NEEDING TO WIN ALL THE TIME
ONLY MAKES YOU A LOSER

I've learned that you can lose an argument or agree to disagree without losing face. You don't always have to be correct. Living with the uncertainty of, *Hmmm, maybe I'm right, maybe I'm not,* can be a good thing, as it keeps us conscious about our thoughts, feelings, and choices. It also stops us before we ever offer a cringeworthy "I told you so" response.

You can also disagree without making someone else wrong. If you need to prove that you are right all the time, it reflects more of an inner need to work on letting go of insecurities rather than reflecting your wisdom and intelligence. Instead, consider the value of trying to *have a generous spirit.* If you can get joy from prioritizing connection over ego, you will be a lot happier.

I know a lot of happily married people, and what seems to unite them is that even though they all argue, they also all seem to do one thing: They have learned to either compromise or let their partners "win" some arguments. Yes, they've simply learned to say, "I'm wrong this time. Sorry." Or, "I hear what you're saying." Or, "You've got a good point." Five simple words that can mean a great deal. Even if you believe your argument was stronger, your relationship is still intact. So, though there are times for disagreements, it's a good idea to choose your battles carefully, as they can come at a cost.

The ability to be wrong or to just not always have to be right or try to prove you're right about everything will go a long way toward making sure that your relationships are more pleasant and will last. It also just feels better. But don't just take my word for it. Try it.

I'd recommend going further with this. Saying just to compromise or to let the other win doesn't seem sufficient, especially if you actually think the other person is wrong. In my life, before I argue, I try to practice this mind hack and ask myself, *Why am I holding onto this? Do I want to be right (or convince someone I am), or do I want to have peace and connection? Even if it won't alter their opinion, do I still want to push my agenda?*

Listening to what someone is saying, acknowledging when the other person has a good point, arguing to learn more rather than to win (especially in a cherished relationship), and expressing your truth are all helpful ways to live a more harmonious life. And it's nice to just be able to have a fun and comforting connection with other people rather than feeling anxious about proving yourself.

Considerable #25

BE A GOLDFISH AND AN ELEPHANT

In the wonderful TV show *Ted Lasso*, the main character, Coach Ted Lasso, calls the football (soccer in America) player Sam to the sidelines after he fails at a practice play and feels dejected. Lasso asks, "You know what the happiest animal on earth is?" When Sam says no, Lasso continues, "It's a goldfish. It's got a ten-second memory. Be a goldfish."

Though it's good to learn from failures and mistakes, it's not healthy to stay stuck in dejection. At one point, after losing a high-stakes game, Coach Lasso also tells the whole team (similar to the It's Okay to be Sad for a While considerable), "Let's be sad now. Let's be sad together. And then we can be a gosh darn goldfish." I thought that was the perfect thing to say to a team suffering the letdown of a devastating loss. Together, they can grieve the loss, and then, rather than staying stuck in upset, they can look forward and work toward the next game and hopeful victory. They need to have a very short memory.

However, with that said, there are also times when it's valuable to have the long-term memory of an elephant. So many students' lives have been positively impacted by a favorite teacher who's had the job of working with students for years, if not decades. Over their careers, those teachers likely have memories of experiences that have informed their instructional skills and allowed them to become more effective with each new class. We can benefit from remembering aspects of the past, especially when we learn from the mistakes we made, so we are not doomed to repeat them. If these teachers had the memory of a goldfish, both about the things they've learned through making mistakes and the things they've succeeded at from the start, they'd be much less adept at what they do. Sometimes the elephant trumps the goldfish.

Thus, the key thing here is to know when to have the memory of a goldfish and when it's best to have the memory of an elephant. To determine this, consider the ramifications of holding on to this memory. If I never forget this, will it help me or hurt me? The answer to this simple question should guarantee that you make the right decision about whether to be an elephant or a goldfish.

Considerable #26

PEOPLE ARE FUNNY

This simple phrase can be immensely valuable for navigating your way through this crazy world. Don't believe me? When someone behaves in a way you find strange, give it a try.

There have been many times when I was upset by, well, let's just say a surprising or unnerving encounter with another human being. When I would tell the story of the encounter to a close friend, she would simply state what I now consider to be the go-to mantra and the perfect non-judgmental expression, "People are *funny*!"

Yes, dear reader, "People *are* funny!"

Think about it. Not "Ha! Ha!" funny, but quirky, weird, and strangely funny. Every one of us has our own unique behaviors and responses that show up in various interactions. Once you accept this, you can much more easily digest others' foibles and frailties and even appreciate how different we all are. You can more readily laugh at how humans are such a strange species, thereby lessening any agitation. You don't have to beat them or yourself up when things go south. So, when you have plans to meet somebody for dinner and then they suddenly just flake, instead of getting angry or going off on a tirade, you might be better served by having a nice meal on your own and saying, "Oh well. People are funny!"

This mantra has saved me in many interactions. For example, an online date never shows up, and I get pissed off. Sure, she's wasted my time, and I want to act out my aggression and send her a nasty text, but saying this mantra is easier and healthier and allows me to let the incident go without having to spend further energy dealing with the upset or any ramifications of my sending a nasty text.

Or when you work really hard on something and share it with a colleague in the office and get no feedback, not even a thanks, don't get mad. You may even think, *I might have responded differently, but so it is*. Then you can just say to yourself, "You know what? People are funny!" Yes. Sometimes it's good to let people off the hook. Because people are funny. So, hopefully, when you do something that another person doesn't fully understand, they'll let you off the hook, knowing that you're a people too.

Considerable #27

LOOK AT YOUR GPS, AND THERE YOU ARE

I have a friend whose wife was never happy. They lived in New England and she hated New England, so they moved up to the Catskill Mountains. But after a year, she found the mountains to be lacking, so they moved to her hometown way down south in order to be close to her family, thinking that would make her happy.

But the reality of living close to her family didn't match her dream either, and she soon grew tired of that location too. Then she grew tired of my friend, and they got divorced.

He and I went out for dinner one night, and I asked him what happened.

He answered, "Wherever we went, she was unhappy. At first I thought moving around might help, but after a while I realized wherever we went, she found fault in that place. Eventually, I realized it wasn't the place, it was her. She took her unhappiness with her, so how could she ever avoid it? She carried it around on her shoulders, and it weighed us both down. Eventually it destroyed us, and the divorce was a blessing."

Wherever your GPS says you are, there you are.

Whatever the circumstances, it's always up to you to make of your situation what you will. You can, at the same time, strive for more while also appreciating what's right here. Your attitude can make the difference in whether a situation will weigh you down or lift you up. Each of us can choose to make things better in our lives, not worse. You're never lost if you're present to yourself. And you can always find yourself right where you are (and feeling grateful for what you have along the way doesn't hurt either).

Considerable #28

TRAVEL MORE, STAY HOME LESS

Though it was originally thought that the brain couldn't evolve after childhood, it's become clear that's not the case. There's even a term for the capacity of the brain to develop new neural pathways and change throughout your life: *neuroplasticity*. If you want to shift any thoughts or behaviors or responses, diminish mental health issues or patterned behaviors that negatively affect your life, create new memories, become more innovative and resourceful, adapt to a situation, learn a new skill, recover from an illness, and/or heal relationships, it should offer hope to know that you can rewire/retrain your brain through new thoughts and experiences. And what better way to infuse your life with novelty than to travel?

Sure, many of us dream of taking an exotic trip, perhaps to Bali or going on safari in Africa or going to see the Northern Lights. But even if you don't have the time or money to go far, travel can be just taking a different route to the corner store and having a conversation with the cashier, or maybe even getting in a van and driving around to a neighborhood or place you've never been to before. The point is, wherever it is you want to travel—whether via a plane, walking, daydreaming, rethinking an idea, reading a book, engaging in a craft, or any other of the diverse ways to experience life—getting out of your comfort zone, especially if you've become habituated to the ease of just staying at home and binge-watching a TV series instead of going anywhere, can be revitalizing and forge new neural pathways to making positive change.

Sure, there are some basic, pretty universal human traits. We have skeletons under our skin and in our closets. We were born and will die. We want to feel safe and secure. And who doesn't love pizza? But we often make assumptions about the world and others, their values and cultures and traditions, and assume our way is the norm or that different means bad. When you travel, you actually begin to discover rather than just assume. Learning new things expands and deepens your understanding of the world, others, yourself, and your own culture. Even if leaving your comfort zone is a tad scary at first, it's worth it. Travel is not only fun and interesting but can increase your openness to life and to more new and expansive experiences while also broadening your capability to adapt.

Life should not be like a driverless car, where we don't forge our own experiences or ever choose in which direction we'll head. But all too often it is, for most of us. I had this revelation recently when I saw a car with the driver literally asleep at the wheel and a passenger apparently asleep as well. Were they some wacky dudes testing a self-driving vehicle? Was the driver just relaxing and working on driving with his feet instead of his hands? Was I just being delusional? Whatever the answer, it got me thinking about how driverless vehicles mimic our lives, all too often surrendering to our autonomic nervous system and living the majority of life on autopilot. We repeat the daily grind day after day, taking much of it for granted while tending to the pressing matters of family and finance instead of trying anything new—even something small, like a food we've never eaten before.

Have you ever been so stressed that you felt you couldn't do one more thing but then were able to get back and capably handle the very same to-dos after simply having a snack, stopping to look at the beauty of a newly emerged flower, daydreaming, curling up with a good book for a bit, taking a walk/run, meditating, or making some other new, temporary excursion away from your task(s)? Making the time for such traveling experiences, whether a few minutes or hours or days, can increase the amount of pleasure you experience and decrease the stress of things that will need doing regardless.

A little while back, I found myself running along a lake on a gorgeous cloud-free day in Hyde Park, London. Only twelve hours earlier, I had been on the freeway in Los Angeles in what seemed a dry, burned-out city of isolated souls and angry motorists. Despite being sleep-deprived and jet-lagged, I was ecstatic to be back in England again, and as I jogged, I saw London in a way I had never seen it before. As I ran through Hyde Park, I wondered, *Why do we travel?*

Have you ever heard the oft-told story of the two fish who are asked by another fish swimming by, "How's the water?" and one looks at the other and asks, "What's water?" I think that we can't *really* see the world around us when it's so familiar. We only know what we know, and the more we experience and learn, the more we will know. When we are home and stuck in our daily routines, we miss out. Though there's a comfort in what's familiar (our personal "normal") and repetition can help us learn, it can also make us fall asleep to what's right in front of or around us. And though familiarity can make it seem like we are safe, it doesn't actually make the world any more controllable or small.

With the eyes of a tourist, you get a new perspective, seeing things as if for the first time, which awakens your senses and helps you feel more alive. You move out of the dull gray into the rich purple of the world. On a deeper level, is this not the reason we are drawn to travel? And is it not also the reason why we appreciate our homes and families so much more upon our return? When we travel, we gain new insights and, therefore, a broader perspective. Might that also be why, when we can't afford to take a week off and go away to a location like Europe, we are still drawn to visit a local museum or gallery?

Travel near, travel far, but either way, it's wise to get out of your routine and change your scenery, even if that just means taking the time to explore your own imagination. A new traveling experience is a way to forge a neural—and literal—pathway to a destination where your life is enriched and you are thriving.

Considerable #29

WE ACTUALLY DO NEED ART TO SURVIVE

S peaking of art and museums… though most of us
would probably agree that art is nice to display on
a wall or shelf or to entertain us, some might not feel
it's essential to existence. Some of you may even be
thinking, *Give me food, shelter, etc. I need those things
to survive, but I don't really need art.*

I disagree. Sure, maybe we could technically
"survive" without art. Maybe we would continue to
breathe even if all art was removed from the world—
if that were even possible. But let's say it was possible,
and you could remove all art and design from nature.
Oh, what an empty existence that would be! For us to
fully exist as human beings, I would argue that *we
need art.*

Think about it.

Well, first of all, what is art?

In the broadest sense of the word, I would posit
that art is anything that comes from the act of creation,
so without it, there'd be only that which was here
before us. One might even argue that if art didn't exist,
neither would we. Without art, there would be no
design, in any form or anywhere. For argument's sake
(because even a design would need to be designed),
let's say there were a basic template for everything.

Even then, without art, all clothes, architecture, meals, etc. would look the same. They—and we—would be indistinguishable without any individual expression. Digging a bit deeper, just consider, for a sec, if all architecture were merely functional and looked exactly alike. Wouldn't our homes and buildings be less inspiring and inviting, less warm and welcoming? Can you imagine if all music sounded the same? Or if there was no opportunity to take photos or see pictures from all around the world? What would you do without books, television, movies, theater, dance? What if everyone looked alike, with the same hairstyles and same exact clothing? Every single day. As long as you live.

Art is so integral to life. Art gives life to life. It evokes diverse emotions and enables their expression. Art brings color to life; it is the purple enlivening the gray. That doesn't always mean it will be awesome and beautiful, because art is about life and life is chock full of yin and yang and diversity. But it expresses the fullness of life.

Is it not through *making art* and *experiencing art* that we are offered a chance to see ourselves and our world in a fresh, new way? Even before writing, people were using art to communicate through cave drawings. At the time, those drawings may have helped with relationships and survival, and now we can still view them in order to learn more about our ancestral past and the history of the world. Art enables expression, celebrates differences *and* similarities, and transcends boundaries.

If everything were the same, it would be familiar, yes, but familiarity can breed more than just contempt; it can also breed a sort of blindness. Think of it like a landfill that overpowers us with its stink when we first enter its confines, but then, after only spending a few minutes there in the putrescence, magically, thankfully, somehow, the smell dissipates until we soon don't even notice it. In a way then, aren't we are all just unconscious dwellers in the landfill of our choosing? Art extracts us from the landfill and brings us into awareness and sensation. It helps us discover and create, so we don't stay (knowingly or unknowingly) stuck in stink.

We can study the neuroscience, but maybe it's not that complicated that we sometimes tone things down and stick with the familiar, asserting that art isn't necessary or that big a deal. Maybe that's why the arts are often the first courses to be cut when schools face budget constraints—despite studies showing that lack of an arts-integrated education may result in diminished proficiency in other subjects and skill sets. Maybe it's just that we live on a planet filled with such overwhelming beauty (because of art in the nature surrounding us as well as art we create) that if we were to spend every moment of every day being awestruck by the grandeur and magnificence of it all, well, life would grind to a deadening halt.

Our brains have, by necessity, been programmed to quickly turn the extraordinary into the familiar, and as a result, we learn to not notice the spectacular splendor that is everywhere and to stop considering how essential and prevalent art is. This thought process is not right or wrong; it's just what we as human beings have been programmed to do over the eons.

I once heard a great quote, "Travel is the only thing that you can buy that truly makes you richer." Well, I'd have to add art to that list as well.

So if you can't travel this week, like I suggested in the previous considerable, at least go look at or listen to or create some art and see your world in a new way. It's because of art that we are able to communicate and express ourselves, to witness and take in the world, and to feel a sense of aliveness. Have you ever witnessed a baby's delight as they discover colors and shapes and textures? Even if you consider yourself a jaded adult, with art you can recapture that sense of pleasure as if for the first time—surrendering to it as you inevitably, slowly, steadfastly fall to your knees and utter short, incoherent mutterings of appreciation.

Considerable #30

CHOOSE TO BE KIND

There are many ways to be kind. Kindness (from the bottom up, top down, or otherwise) can involve simply having a caring, respectful, compassionate attitude, or being friendly and considerate of others, or taking action and doing someone a good turn or favor. Kindness is a function of consciousness and choice and a beneficial habit that is well worth forming. Did you know that oxytocin— the feel-good hormone that gets released when you do things like fall in love, hug/kiss, have sex, play with your pets, meditate, do yoga, and listen to your favorite music—also gets released when you are kind (or treated kindly)?

A search online will lead you to several links which show scientific arguments for kindness. Yes, it does more than just feel good to you. It is good for you. At the time this book went to press, information about proven benefits of kindness could be found on numerous sites online. These included blog sites such as Cedars Sinai ("Science of Kindness") and Harvard ("The Heart and Science of Kindness") and websites like that of Dr. David Hamilton ("The 5 Side Effects of Kindness"), the Mayo Clinic ("Practice the Art of

Kindness"), and the Random Acts of Kindness Foundation.

Okay, let me tell you a story that explores this considerable further. I had bought some vegan cheese that was supposed to taste like a smoked-salmon-flavored cream cheese spread. I love cream cheese and lox and was excited about it, so I bought two containers of it. Unfortunately, when I got home and tried this product, it was nasty. It was on the verge of being out of date, and well, I guess vegan lox spread is just a bad idea.

Either way, it just wasn't something I could eat, so I brought it back to the grocery store and asked to speak to the manager. I told him that I didn't like it and asked for store credit so I could get something else.

He laughed at me and sneered, "Just because you don't like something doesn't mean you can return it."

I argued, "Well, I kinda thought your store's goal is to have happy customers, and I'm not exactly happy with this product. I don't know if it's bad because it's out of date or just a bad product, but either way, it's not edible."

He walked away and chortled, "Sorry. Can't do it just because you didn't like it."

I felt belittled. Scorned. Condescended to. I wanted to say something, do something, lash out and reaffirm my manhood and sense of self. Yes, it was only like seven bucks in store credit, but still, I believed he should've handled the situation differently and not embarrassed and alienated me in front of everybody else in the store.

The only thing I felt I could do at that point was either to be an angry customer and yell more or to choose a kinder route, which, as I saw it, meant not to yell or act out in any way. To deal with my emotions and act civilized.

I harrumphed to myself and nodded and walked away. I swallowed my pride and ate my seven-dollar loss. Life's too short to get bent out of shape over seven dollars, right? Sure, he could've treated me more respectfully, especially since businesses want repeat customers, but what can you do?

I still had some grocery shopping to do. So I went down the produce aisle and got some fresh greens. I was still a bit upset, but I tried not to think about it. I bought what I needed, paid for it, and I left.

The following day I returned to the store to get a few more items that I had purchased, really liked, and wanted more of. Upon paying for them, I realized that I didn't have my credit card. The slot in my wallet— where it always is—was empty. It was just gone. Poof! Oh my God! What a horrible feeling!

I knew I'd used it in this grocery store the day before, but since then I'd somehow lost it. I stumbled out to the car and left the parking lot. While I was driving away I realized maybe I had been so upset the day before that I'd left it in the credit card machine instead of removing it. So I turned around and returned to the store.

I parked (again), went into the store (again), and approached (again) the very same manager who had ridiculed me the day before. I told him that I thought I'd left my credit card there yesterday. He asked me my name and went into his office to check. Voila! There it was. Yay!

He was kind and friendly and returned it to me. Because of that, I breathed a deep sigh of relief. I even checked on the card, and it hadn't been used in the past twenty-four hours. It was a strange sequence of events, but in the end, I believe that my act of kindness in not arguing was then rewarded by his act of kindness the following day. In being kind, we both ended up avoiding a more uncomfortable and potentially more volatile situation.

You don't know what's been going on in someone's life or mind or heart that might affect how they're acting or responding in a particular moment. Might that guy have just been yelled at by a supervisor or another shopper? Perhaps he'd had an argument with his spouse that morning or felt a headache coming on. Sure, it's easy to act out of anger and to lash out at people when your feelings are hurt, but why not choose to be kind, to be civil and respectful? And in this situation, I'm awfully glad I did.

Allow me to illustrate this precept a bit more with another story. I've done my share of online dating. One night, I was scanning an online dating app, and lo and behold, a friend's wife appeared. I quickly checked Facebook to see if they had divorced. And, nope, they were still together. Please note, they live in California, many miles away from me, and she was showing up as a single lady in a beach city right down the road from me. She wasn't using the travel mode of the app. She listed her hometown as another city, where they did not live. She was literally in a hotel room or bar close to me. I freaked out and quickly swiped left so she wouldn't see me on the app and in order to avert a potentially embarrassing situation.

But then questions plagued me for days. What to do? Should I contact my buddy and tell him? Maybe they have an open marriage and I didn't know about it. I reached out to him to see how he was doing, and he told me all was well. Hmmm. So many questions. What did I owe my friend? Was it any of my business? Would I hurt him if I told him about my discovery? Was it my moral obligation to do so? On and on, the questions bounced around in my mind.

What to do? What's the right thing to do? I didn't really know (can anyone really know?), but in the end, it seemed the kindest thing to do was to keep my mouth shut and let it go. Saying something could have some massive consequences, and I chose to mind my own business. I know very little about their personal relationship and agreements, and the hurt and pain I could bring my friend seemed to outweigh everything else. So I kept it to myself and chose what I felt to be kindness over complete honesty concerning a situation I really knew little about.

Maybe you think I did the wrong thing, but I would rather live with the knowledge and not hurt my friend than to hurt him by telling him what I saw. This also demonstrates that even though kindness may seem to be obvious or a simple thing to practice, it's not always so clear or easy to do in every case. In the end, regardless of whether what I did was right or wrong (and I'm sure you can find valid arguments on both sides), to me I chose what felt more kind—to not interfere in a relationship that isn't mine.

Many times in life we want to act in a way that makes ourselves feel better, but I would argue that sometimes the kindest thing to do is to act in a way that, to the best of your ability, ensures you are not hurting someone else. Though it's not always 100 percent clear what that might be, perhaps the best place to start is by taking a moment (with loving intention) to think not about how your action will affect you but how it might affect others. As they say in the medical field from the very start of care, "First, do no harm."

Considerable #31

DO SOMETHING WITH YOUR LIFE

Poet Mary Oliver once said, "What is it you plan to do with your one wild and precious life?"

It's a lovely question. As far as we know, we have one go at this life, so of course it's precious. And with all the unknowns, it also contains lots of wild. So then, may I ask, have you thought at all about what you are doing with yours?

Later in this book I write about the benefit of farting around, and there are times when that's helpful, even necessary. But over the course of your entire life, it's also sometimes helpful, even necessary, to get a move on and take action. In fact, maybe the ideas of what to do will come to you while you're farting around. What have you done up to now, and should you be doing anything different from now on?

A good way to think about this concept was articulated by the late Dr. David Viscott, a popular radio therapist, who once said, "The purpose of life is to discover your gift. The work of life is to develop it. The meaning of life is to give your gift away."

This is one of my favorite quotes of all time. It encompasses the whole human life cycle. It's broad enough to be inclusive of us all. It's just so wise and inspiring. If we spend our younger years discovering our gifts and then the majority of our lives developing our gifts, once we've achieved a certain degree of mastery, what better thing is there to do than to find meaning in sharing those gifts with the world?

What a great way to avoid the hollowness and nihilism of existence. It's a perfect win-win. Put in your ten thousand hours (as referenced in Malcolm Gladwell's book *Outliers: The Story of Success,* which suggests that's the time it takes to become expert in a skill) and develop yourself. Get good at something and make a life for yourself doing what you enjoy. Having a sense of purpose can really help you navigate through some of the gray areas, right?

We all know somebody who seemed lost and then found a passion. I have a college friend who always felt compelled to have a big, seemingly important job, owing to his Yale degree. But you know what? He wasn't happy. All he ever really wanted to do was make pizzas. The guy really loved pizza. He spent all his spare time searching for the best flour and dough and sauce and pizza recipes. In fact, his homemade pizza recipe became the number one, most-liked online recipe in the world at the time. He was obsessed and knew he needed to figure out how to take his oven up to 900 degrees to simulate a coal-fired oven. So he even rigged the self-cleaning element of his oven to go above the 500-degree limit, and while putting in his ten thousand hours, he eventually destroyed several ovens trying to make the perfect pizza.

Finally, in his forties, he quit his job and did the unthinkable. He opened a pizza parlor, and it was daunting and a big risk (as new ventures and opening any kind of restaurant can be). But his pizzas were a big hit. Today, he makes a good living making pizzas. Most importantly, he's the happiest he's ever been. When you find your purpose and lean into it, it can bring more contentment and richness to your life.

And then, as Dr. Viscott said, at a certain point, don't forget to also give back. That doesn't necessarily mean monetarily. You can give back with your time or expertise or help in any way that seems right to you. The main thing is that it feels good to try to master something, and then, once that happens, it also feels good to help others gain mastery too.

Everyone's "something" will be different, and trying something is the first step to finding yours. Psychotherapist C.G. Jung put it well in a letter to a struggling patient when he said, "Nobody can set right a mismanaged life with a few words. But there is no pit you cannot climb out of, provided you make the right effort at the right place."

Considerable #32

WHAT PEOPLE SAY ABOUT YOU
IS REALLY MORE ABOUT THEM

I know a lot of people who make all their choices based upon what other people might think. Their thinking goes something like this: *I like these shoes, but will people make fun of me if I wear them? I love musicals, but what will my buddies say if I tell them? I want to dance, but will I look too foolish?*

As I illustrated in the opening paragraphs of this book, there are places with set rules and cultures, such as a golf course, which help maintain a respectful sense of community. And, fortunately, for those of us still living in a free country, there's a lot of opportunity for self-expression in most aspects of life these days. Even on a golf course with a strict dress code, you can still wear loud, flowery prints or more subdued plaids. It's your choice. In a world trying to make us the same, we are all unique individuals.

The issue here is simply that when people pass judgements—for example, when they say something like, "Oh my God, I can't believe you're wearing that outfit!"—we often take it personally and end up feeling badly about ourselves or them. I included the earlier chapter about the importance of leaving the judging to others so you can focus on your life and avoid that negativity. It's a concept worth repeating, and this chapter talks about why that's so.

So let's go deeper. As this considerable suggests, judgements made by other people are not about you. They are statements of *their* needs and wants and beliefs and values (whether based on their own thinking or their trying to impress someone else or fit a cultural norm)—*not yours*. If you're on the golf course and the rules dictate you need to wear a collared shirt and you choose one with pink flamingoes on it, you may be making your own statement, but if others don't like your choice, well, then that's about them and their tastes and ideas, not you or yours.

Sure, maybe they wouldn't wear a top like that, but if you want to, go for it. You like your style, and it's not harming anyone else. When people comment on the way you are choosing to live your life, their comments are reflections of how they want or think they should live their lives, not on how you should live yours. Who is the great determiner of who you are and ought to be? Only you can be. Sometimes that means exploring until things feel right—for you.

I know that when I started re-contextualizing what other people said to me, especially the negative comments, and started reading them as merely comments about the person who was delivering them, my life became a lot easier. I felt that a sort of burden had been lifted, and I no longer carry the issues of others as if they're mine or take on their comments as if they know more about me than I know about myself. And so, when someone criticizes one of my paintings or an outfit I'm wearing, instead of getting defensive or upset, I try to rise above my initial emotional response and explore what I think their criticism says about them. In doing so, I don't internalize the critique and it gets defused.

Have you ever heard of Abe Maslow's hierarchy of needs? It begins with the basic human essentials, like food and shelter, and moves all the way up to what he described as the highest form of human need, self-actualization. If you are reading this book, most likely your basic needs are covered. Lucky you. With that taken care of, you can then strive to become fully realized and self-actualized as a human being. Knowing other people's judgements are about them, you can strive to move beyond what others think of you and do what you think you need to do to become the best, most fully realized person you can be. And in doing so, you will probably feel a lot more fulfilled in your life.

Considerable #33

DO ART FOR YOURSELF

It is great to make a living as an artist. That said, if you haven't already guessed from my chapter on how art is essential, I believe that everybody should (and does) create in some way or another. Whether you paint or act or write or dance or sing/play music or whatever artistic pursuit you love, consider doing it for yourself. Allow yourself to explore in a way that is not soul-crushing. Express yourself using your unique voice. Whatever you do with your life, make time to do some act of creation that nourishes your soul. And then, don't connect that art to a monetary gain. In other words, just because nobody buys your paintings or your band isn't getting any bookings or you can't get your novel published, you shouldn't downplay the value of your time spent doing your chosen art form. You're doing it because you love it. There's rich reward in the pleasure of the process.

How this plays out in real life is simply this: Disconnect from results with your art.

Here's what I've discovered has made a profound difference for me. Don't put pressure on yourself to achieve at a professional level at first and maybe ever. Instead, do what fills your soul with pleasure, whether you then decide to put it in your drawer or share it with the world. Maybe the world will shower you with praise or disdain or money. Or maybe the world will ignore you. Don't measure the value of what you do in likes or dollars. Measure it in how it makes you feel to do it.

There are Zen monks who spend all week, hours every day, making incredible multi-colored mandalas out of sand. At the end of the week, when the mandalas are finished, there is a short ceremony that ends with the monks sweeping the sand off into the wind as a symbol of life's impermanence. They destroy their art that they've spent dozens of hours creating.

Does that idea seem outrageous? Well, people are funny…. But in this case, sweeping away their art is the embodiment of their practice of non-attachment. Be present as you create, and then enjoy the moment. Then, let go of any ties to what you create. Send it into the wind. Enjoy the process. Be still.

Whatever your equivalent of the monks' mandala, just recognize that the pursuit of your chosen art form is really just for you. For example, I like to paint. Sometimes I sell my paintings. Sometimes I don't. But I love doing it, so I do it. I also give my paintings away to people I care about. And I am fortunate to have a job that pays the rent. This allows me to engage in doing the art that I love for myself, and that keeps me happy.

Protect the pleasure you get from creating, and disconnect your art from anything but continuing your contentment. You don't need justification or an audience to create. The doing is enough if it is a process that brings you meaning, joy, and/or gratification.

Considerable #34

SEE A CHRISTMAS CAROL EVERY YEAR

Many theaters show the Charles Dickens' play *A Christmas Carol* on their stages every year. And you know what? They sell out every year as well.

I have a theory about why people go back to see that same play year after year. Dickens' story is maybe the best example ever written of a human being going from being totally selfish to totally selfless in one night. And haven't we all, at some point in our lives, wished for redemption after doing or saying something or many things we regret?

The ghosts that haunt the play's cruel protagonist, Ebenezer Scrooge, force him to look at the choices he has made in his life, and as a result, he grows and changes. Think of it as the greatest one-night talk therapy session in literature.

I have come to believe that so many of us see this show to tap into something deep in our souls. All of us can become a bit Scrooge-like during the year. It is natural. Life, year-round, has a lot of stresses. The world is constantly bombarding us with expectations and to-dos and people and causes wanting our time, energy, and/or money. The onslaught seems to be never-ending. We shut down. We become irritated and irritable. We can survive the onslaught only by becoming, well, a bit selfish. We close our hearts. We push forward and turn away from homeless people begging for money. We forget to be kind.

And then, when Christmas time comes around and we see this stage show (or re-watch the movie), we are reminded of the value and import of having a spirit of goodwill toward our fellow man. We reconnect with the generosity of our souls, as does Scrooge, and we leave the theater feeling renewed. We feel better about ourselves. We act more generously again when we interact with others.

That is, of course, until the onslaught becomes overwhelming again and life catches up with us over the next twelve months, until we go see the play/movie again and reconnect with our humanity one more time. Is it really so surprising that Ebenezer Scrooge (or in another holiday example, the Grinch)—who originally couldn't stand to see others being jubilant while celebrating together—finds himself fitting in, belonging with those he originally belittled, finding joy from having acted in a way that opened/expanded his heart? This is a show that's worth its message weight in gold.

Considerable #35

BE OPEN

It's easy to say no. It's easy to get into a routine and want to shut out the world. And sometimes, if feels safer to do so, when the din of the world is so loud that we need some space in order to refuel and renew.

In general, though, I hope you can resist this urge if it arises frequently. So much of life (especially the best parts) is unplanned or unexpected or outside of our daily routine purview. And you can only profit from such turns of events if you are open to the world, if you are willing to say yes instead of "No, sorry, I can't" and making excuses not to engage. Let me share two stories with you to illustrate this considerable.

First, a personal story. Over the past thirty-five years, I have been fortunate to make a living creating narratives across different genres—fiction and nonfiction, stage plays, and screenplays. In addition, I've been a professor of dramatic writing in the undergraduate and graduate classrooms of USC Cinema School, UCLA Film School, Emerson College, and Ithaca College. From there, I started lecturing to aspiring storytellers at writer's conferences and film festivals around the country.

At these conferences, a few writers who heard my lectures started hiring me to privately consult with them on their stories. For years, this was my focus. I wrote, taught, and coached writers, but still, all that time, I was struggling to make a living. Then, one day, I was asked to be one of the featured speakers at a conference on storytelling that was several hours away from my home in Los Angeles. There was no pay for the presenters, and I was required to cover all of my travel, meal, and hotel expenses over the course of the weekend. At that time, since I was still struggling as a freelancer, I always needed to keep my eyes out for more clients and work.

The conference was right in my wheelhouse on storytelling, and I wanted to go and share my skills and tricks of the trade with a specific audience that was seeking help with manifesting their aspirations. At the same time, I thought it would be a well-attended conference that would help build my storytelling lecturing business by reaching those in the industry who wanted to hire experienced teachers of the craft.

I decided it was worth the financial risk to spend the money and agreed to participate.

When I walked up to the podium, I looked out at the audience. Damn! Only twelve people showed up for my lecture in a room that seated two hundred. The empty space in the room felt chasmic. Though I gave it my all and the talk went well, it was admittedly a bit deflating. Despite being excited to present and grateful for the positive response from those who did attend, I confess I felt an initial sense of disappointment in being able to share my passion with only twelve people, none of whom approached me that day about my story consulting services. I drove back to Los

Angeles and tried to forget about it. It was a great opportunity to be a goldfish.

Then, a few days later, I got a call from one of the other speakers at the conference, a leading storytelling expert in Hollywood. She said she'd recently gotten a call from a major global brand that wanted to fly her to an exotic foreign country to teach a week-long seminar on storytelling. Though she wished she could go, she already had a booking that week. She conveyed that she had been one of the twelve attendees at my lecture and that she'd recommended me for the job. She wanted to know whether I was interested in talking with them.

Was I interested? Yes! Her recommendation led to my getting not only that job but a whole series of jobs with that company as well as with other companies. In fact, it jump-started a whole new path in my career—helping businesses and entrepreneurs to achieve and sustain greater success with storytelling. And it was all because I presented at that one conference.

We are always writing our own stories in our head, and the story I had been writing in mine was short-sighted. I had come to believe that since I had spent a good deal of time and money on the conference and hadn't gotten a large audience or any immediate consulting jobs from it, it wasn't worthwhile. Well, that story turned out to be erroneous! The lesson to me was abundantly clear: Remain open to opportunities and possibilities, even when outcomes don't seem to go the way you think they should.

Often in life, we don't know what will come from our efforts. We may think we know or try to anticipate outcomes, but we are often pleasantly surprised, especially if we don't close down. Even though there were only twelve people in the audience, I still gave 110 percent in my lecture. As it turned out, one of those twelve people was impressed enough that she recommended me for a job, which ended up changing the course of my life. If I had said no to participating in the event or presenting to so small a crowd, that never would have happened.

So I rewrote my story in my head and learned a good lesson. When you stay open to possibility and do the best you can, you never know how your efforts might have a positive impact on others and, in turn, on your own life. There is always a chance that the person you are sitting next to in a workshop, on a plane, or in a restaurant, for example, could be instrumental in furthering you along an exciting new path in your life. But you have to be in those places and enter conversations in order for that possibility to occur.

Here's another example, a story about my friend Hank. Hank is a great golfer, and when we were golfing one day, he told me this tale. It begins when he was a much younger man and newly married. He was a physical education teacher and not making much money. One weekend he was playing golf and stumbled upon a threesome of strangers who weren't going very quickly. He caught up to them and asked if he could pass. He was about to participate in the state amateur championship tournament and needed to practice. The group turned to him and asked, "Instead of passing us, why don't you join us?"

Hank demurred. He needed to get more practice in. He started to walk away, and then a little voice inside him told him to stop. He decided to join them. For the next few hours, they golfed and chatted. The older gentlemen in the group were so impressed with his golf play and his personality that they invited him to join them in the clubhouse for dinner. They chatted more, and Hank expressed his frustration with being a gym teacher and the low pay. As he spoke, the men just listened. By the end of the evening, they told him that they ran an international car parts company and were looking for a young person such as himself to run their American office. Hank was thrilled to hear it and said he'd like to interview for the job. They laughed and said he didn't have to.

Hank was confused. What did he do wrong?

They said that they had spent the day interviewing him, and he already had the job if he wanted it. He was hired on the spot and went on to have a successful career with them. His life had changed on a dime—or perhaps I should say on the green of hole number seven. And all because Hank was open to the opportunity that arose in front of him. He said yes to their proposal of joining them, and the rest is history.

Remember, you might be in a rush and looking down, but if you take time to slow down and look up, who knows what opportunities might be right in front of you if only you are open to seeing them and saying yes.

Considerable #36

WE ARE HERE TO HELP OTHER PEOPLE

As you probably know by now from reading this book, I've spent most of my professional career writing, striving to make a living doing what I love, and teaching in Hollywood, California. In over three decades of doing this, I've been grateful to have learned a few things. One of my takeaways became clearer while I was pondering this issue: What do we as human beings owe other human beings?

I believe in kindness and try to practice it, but (a) it's not always easy, and (b) Hollywood is not always exactly what you would call a kind place. People tend to be there to become famous, and like most businesses, it is very transactional—the opposite, as you already read, of offering kindness or doing good simply to do good. Many people who I originally believed to be my friends didn't treat me well while I was struggling to make a name for myself, and sometimes people I didn't know or hardly knew treated me better than my friends. The highly transactional atmosphere of Hollywood can be seen when an agent, for example, helps you and gets a percentage of your fee as a result. This is clearly articulated in a contract, so not a surprise, but I did have a few surprises in my career.

My favorite surprise was a moment with a wonderful director by the name of Craig Clyde. Craig has directed many films but is not a "Hollywood" guy in that he's a Mormon who lives in Utah and writes and directs films there. When I was struggling to direct my first film, Craig went out of his way to help me. I mean, totally above and beyond. He would give me free advice and notes on my material, and when I became a director, he invited me to his set to watch and learn from him as he directed. He even let me stay in his home during the shoot.

I was so moved by Craig's efforts on my behalf that I asked him point blank, "Sorry if this sounds rude, but may I ask why are you helping me? You hardly know me."

He answered, "Aren't we all put here to help other people?"

We are here to help other people. I loved that. And isn't it a wonderful credo to live by? Instead of owing each other, we help each other. We are not here solely to help ourselves, but to care about and help others too. Next time you are anxious and absorbed with your own problems, might you be better served by offering help to someone else in need?

This elevates the Be Kind considerable to the next level, with the addition of taking some action. What are a few of the ways you can help others? Be compassionate. Volunteer for a local benefit event. Make a donation, whether of money, clothing/housewares, your time, etc. Listen with presence. Offer to accompany or drive someone to an appointment they may not want to go to alone. Share some items from your garden. Send a handwritten get-well or I-miss-you or I'm-thinking-about-you card in the mail. Offer to babysit or care for a pet of a neighbor who's experiencing some overwhelm (maybe they're working hard for a promotion, or going through a divorce or some medical procedure, or their baby isn't yet sleeping through the night). Add your child's favorite food or a special note of love when you pack their school lunch. Call your parent(s) just to see how they're doing. Make time to be together.

Genuinely helping others helps you feel better. This is not a new concept, though we tend to lose sight of it in the hectic nature of daily living. After all, wasn't it Charles Dickens who said, "No one is useless in this world who lightens the burdens of another."?

Considerable #37

BE YOUR OWN ADVOCATE

I was reminded of how essential it is to be your own advocate in terms of your health, and your life in general, when I received a message from a dear friend, a chemist with a PhD, in England. The ultimate point I take from her story is that no matter who you are or what your background, education, connections, and circumstances are, there are times when we all need to speak up for ourselves. In her case, it saved her life. This was her message:

Here is a cautionary tale… This brief history also illustrates how doctors in the USA and UK kill about 250,000 people every year with their errors.

All symptoms were gastro, so I and the doctors assumed it was Salmonella or Norovirus. Symptoms got worse so I went to the ER at the John Radcliffe—the second-best hospital in the UK, and in Oxford, so apparently has some talented physicians there. They diagnosed "viral gastroenteritis" and sent me home. No Covid test and no tests of any kind.

I got worse and worse. Unimaginable pain, vomiting, etc. Nothing respiratory. My husband and I started emailing everybody we knew for help and answers. And then, a nephrologist named Prof. Cunningham picked up the labs that I had emailed and said he had seen a case similar to mine several years ago, and he would treat me. He worked out of two hospitals but still no bed until Wednesday 24th, am in the morning.

Meanwhile, my husband is exceptionally health anxious, so he was frantic. Tuesday night things went downhill fast, and we called 911 at 3am Wednesday morning—the pain had increased and was now also thoracic, so I was having problems breathing.

The paramedics were great. They did several ECGs to rule out ischemic attack. They said, "We can blue light you to the John Radcliffe or the cardio unit at two other close hospitals so you will at least get some meds within the hour."

I said, "Will I be seen by anyone before 9am?"

They said, "Probably not."

So, much to my husband's horror, I said I wouldn't go to the ER, and I'd go for Professor Cunningham and my bed in critical care in London, instead, in a few hours. (My husband was convinced I'd have a heart attack before 9am.)

That decision saved my life. It was a brave decision under stress and brain fog, and my husband thought it was crazy. Professor Cunningham immediately started an aggressive protocol to reduce the calcium to save my life. I was in critical care for two weeks. My blood calcium had nearly returned to normal levels when I was discharged.

If I hadn't been admitted when I was and it wasn't diagnosed as quickly as Professor Cunningham diagnosed it and treated as aggressively as he did, I wouldn't have lived. It was a window of only a few days. We make our own luck.

I was wowed by her story and how her decision, advocating for herself in such dire circumstances, saved her. It's a reminder that we always need to trust ourselves enough to feel empowered to speak up and take part in making informed decisions about things that affect our lives. To be fair, as someone who is a PhD, she did have an advantage with knowledge, access, and relationships that many of us don't have at the ready. But she also lucked out with the doctor who picked up the labs she had chosen to send when seeking help (and who ultimately saved her life), and she followed her instinct to wait and be seen by him rather than going to another hospital (the only option presented to her at the time). I think it's also fair to say that no matter what level of knowledge and education we might have, we can all learn to advocate for ourselves. Nobody knows your body better than you do, and you're the one who is left living with the decision. After all, unless they're someone who lives with you, your doctor won't come home with you.

Advocating for yourself is not restricted to the medical realm and it does not mean you ignore others' wisdom or input. Instead, it is participating in what affects your life, understanding and effectively communicating your needs (respectfully, being able to assert your rights and negotiate (as needed), and in so doing, seeking to obtain something (like a promotion or even just being more comfortable in a situation) or to reverse or prevent harm or inequity. Even in situations where you don't have preordained knowledge or connections, you can convey what you do/don't like or want or need. You can also gather essential information, ask for support, speak up, or seek answers to questions so you can make better-informed decisions on your own behalf. There are myriad examples of situations where this is beneficial, including (but definitely not limited to):

• Someone with a disability advocating for their right to easier and equal access;

• Asking for a raise or inquiring about taking on more responsibility or discovering where you can obtain more training to further your career;

• Requesting more time for a school assignment or offering your input in a group project;

• Sharing about—rather than suppressing or denying—a personal struggle, and, if needed, asking for help (This could be as simple as help lifting a heavy package or complex as dealing with mental health issues and so much more);

• Making time for yourself to rest and renew and/or saying no (Have you ever been overloaded and exhausted but still said yes to requests that came your way, such as taking on another project or committee assignment, baking cookies that are needed tomorrow for your kids' school, going out when you'd rather stay in and recuperate, etc.?);

• Stating your preferences when it comes to different relationships (e.g.: providing your input when deciding where to go for a meal or a night out or a vacation, setting terms for a partnership, personal or business or even a divorce settlement).

If advocating for yourself doesn't come easily to you (for whatever reasons), keep in mind that it's a skill you can learn, especially the more you practice. It's well worth it for your own sanity, safety, ease, and pleasure, even if the response isn't always what you hope for. If it's easiest to dip one toe in the water, perhaps start with defining what is important to you in a particular situation and then take the next step of asking for help or offering your input.

One last thought on the subject of self-advocacy: Though it's vital to be self-aware and it enriches our lives to be able to communicate and speak up, when doing so it's also important to keep in mind the considerable Choose to Be Kind—and that means to yourself as well as others.

Considerable #38

FART AROUND

The late author Kurt Vonnegut was interviewed by David Brancaccio decades ago on PBS (Public Broadcasting System). In the interview, he tells a story about going out to buy a single envelope, even though his wife had suggested he should just buy a hundred of them and store them in the closet to avoid having to go out every time he needs one. But Vonnegut asserts that it's the process of going out and meeting people, seeing dogs and fire engines, interacting with the world, and being a "dancing animal" that is the reason for living. He says that we are here to "fart around," and when we realize that the farting around is really an important aspect of our existence, then our life becomes endowed with more meaning.

He goes on to warn that computers will keep us from our natural inclination to be moving and dancing and engaged with the world. In this age of social media trolls and the growing rates of addiction to our screens, his words now appear to have been prophetic.

When I consider Vonnegut's words, I think he was conveying that as you get older, you realize small talk really isn't small and that having a sense of wonder and going out wandering without a specific plan or purpose is time well spent! The "small" interactions of our daily existence, when we're just moving through life, are what define us and give us our humanity.

This is something that has been gaining attention in several cultures as a means to self-care and well-being. For example, in France, they talk about the art of *flaneuring*, intentional wandering, and in Denmark, there is the art of *niksen*, the Dutch solution to being too busy by simply being idle. I also see it as similar to the Buddhist concept of non-attachment, being disconnected from end results and more present in the moment.

In an age when lots of the big stuff is no longer sacred and religion doesn't seem to provide the answers, what happens if we consider that maybe the answers exist in the moments in between all of the fussing and have-tos? Where we make time to simply wander and notice and engage with what is, and where we can discover the actual sacredness in life without needing a prescribed end result.

Considerable #39

I DON'T KNOW WHAT I'M DOING, LIKE EVER

I love reading bios of people on online dating sites. Most people focus on the pictures, and of course, they're fascinating, too, but I tend to focus on what they choose to write. You can learn so much about another human being by how they present their bio, especially when they only have a limited number of words to choose from.

My favorite bio ever was short and sweet. It simply stated, "I don't know what I'm doing. Like ever."

This is the ultimate down on your knees, surrender to the forces at work in our world submission to life. I like to think of it as a modern-day interpretation of Socrates' famous aphorism, "I know that I know nothing." Plato famously captured Socrates saying this in regard to what passed for knowledge among the supposedly wise men of their time. Then there's what William Goldman said about Hollywood: "Nobody knows nothing."

This is such an important concept. The moment we acknowledge that we really don't know anything, like ever, we are suddenly open to the world and opportunities around us. Once we stop trying so hard to label and control everything, we can just experience the here and now. When we're present, we become more aware. We see and feel more. We are suddenly alive and receptive and ready to learn again, child-like with wonder. We are not self-judgmental or feeling pressured to be an expert, so we are not closed off to the world. Instead, we are unjaded and can move in whatever direction we are meant to go next. And isn't that the most fantastic place to be?

I've experienced this often. For example, many times when I am teaching writing, I will read a student's work in advance and not immediately know how to respond to it. I used to panic and worry that once class started, I'd have nothing insightful and helpful to offer them, but alas, every time class would begin and we'd start to discuss the piece, valuable feedback would inevitably come to and pour out of me. I really don't know how it works, but it always seems to happen, so perhaps the big lesson is that we may not always feel like we know what we're doing in the moment, but if we trust ourselves to figure it out and not get in our own way, more often than not, we'll find a workable answer.

If this is of interest to you, give it a try. Next time you're in a situation where you don't know how to proceed, don't force it, just admit you don't know, give in to the not knowing, and see what happens.

Considerable #40

SEE BEYOND THE TRIBE AND THE RACE, AND FOCUS ON THE HUMAN

In this divided age, when people choose to interact with their phones versus connecting in person, I think it's worth making a conscious choice to take some time each day to look beyond that small screen. There are lots of studies out there that show the deep correlation between human connection/interaction and health/longevity.

In this age where we all are connected and interact technologically, maybe the best thing for us to aspire to is making more effort and time to connect and interact *without* technology. To try to connect directly with other people, other humans. Frankly, I don't like the term *human race*. When I hear it, I think of us all on a track, pitted against each other, racing and competing to see who can win. Shouldn't the human experience be thought of as something different than a race?

So, as I end this book, I want to ask one thing: Can we stop thinking of ourselves as only members of a certain category, a specific identity marker, like our religion or nationality? Can we agree that, at the most fundamental level, we're *all* just human beings who have similar core needs, such as sharing resources, like the air we breathe, the water we drink and use, and the land we live on in order to survive? Can we engage in a human collaboration or a collective human sharing instead of a deadly, competitive human race?

Like I discussed earlier with Maslow's hierarchy of needs, we all need/want similar basic things, no matter how different we may seem on the surface. Yes, we all want safety and security, to be fed and sheltered, to protect our families, and to feel good about ourselves. I could go on and on.... Regardless of our differences, we share those core human values, and I think it's important to focus on those.

The issue becomes this: Over the course of the human experience, sometimes our core values might overlap or even contradict the core values of another human. And hence, inevitable conflict arises. However, I would argue that if we all subscribe to and follow the same rules of "et-kit" and regard the well-being of others as equal to our own, maybe we can all co-exist more happily, peacefully, and healthfully and be empowered to be better versions of ourselves.

Finally, I want to share one last aspect of the color purple with you. Online at Britannica.com, there's mention of how the word *purple* may have originated from a shellfish dye (Tyrian purple), which makes me think of how pearls are formed over time in oysters through chafing and the irritation of existence. For me, these 40 considerables have been great antidotes to some of life's irritating and discomfiting aspects. So now that they're in your hands, it's my hope that you will consider implementing any or all of these 40 considerables in your life and see what might be transformed for you. Who knows? Hopefully they'll make a considerable difference by helping you cultivate your own version of an organic gem, a colorful and gratifying end result to having found ways to navigate the gray and less pleasurable areas of life.

End Note

FOUR BONUS CONSIDERABLES

Native American and Canadian First Nation Peoples have been teaching and living a wealth of hard-earned wisdom for centuries, so I thought it would be fitting to end this book of considerables that have shaped my life by honoring some of their ancient teachings.

One wisdom tradition that I'm especially fond of is that of the Cree people. An old friend of mine studied with a storyteller from this tribe, and she taught him about their wisdom traditions. As the aforementioned Dr. Viscott suggested, my friend passed his learnings on to me, and I am passing them on to you.

This nation doesn't have Ten Commandments as in the Judeo-Christian tradition. The Cree people also didn't originally have a written tradition, so they don't have a bible or other sacred texts to refer to. However, they did have a tribal storyteller who was the repository of all the ancient wisdom and narratives of their people. I've always loved the fact that this individual was considered to be the most respected individual in the tribe. He wasn't the greatest warrior or the richest man in the tribe, but he was held in greatest esteem. So, when they wanted to know how to act, they would consult with the tribal storyteller who would share a story with them to provide guidance.

And thus, as I end this book, I, too, want to share with you the four tenets, or considerables, of the Cree people as shared by my friend. I always end my lectures with these four, and so I thought it would be fitting to also end my book with them.

1. Learn something new each day.
2. Teach something new each day to someone else.
3. Do something kind for another human being—without them knowing it—each day.
4. Treat all living things with respect all of the time.

These beliefs, like the ideas put forth in this book, may (once again) be simple but not easy to follow. I feel like I don't need to explain the first two concepts, but the last two are worth explicating a bit.

The third is wonderful, especially in this day and age of social media. I love the fact that hundreds of years ago, the Cree Nation's leaders added the caveat to do good deeds without others knowing about them. This is what I call "the anonymous addendum."

Do good for the sake of doing good and not for any reward. There's no need to brag to get kudos or acknowledgement. Sure, it's wonderful to see someone's face light up when you do a kind act for them, but this should not be the purpose of doing good. You'll know what you've done, and that is rewarding in itself. And can a good deed occur today without someone bragging about it on social media? Test it out for yourself. Try to just do a good deed simply for the sake of doing the right thing. See how it feels in your own personal experience.

And then, the final Cree Nation tenet is one that can't be stressed enough. In our day and age, for some people it's easy to pledge to treat other people well but then not treat animals or other creatures well. We have prioritized our species above all others. The Cree People didn't—and don't—do such a thing. They have always thought of—and still think of—all living things as important and sacred and have treated them as such. How much better would our world be if we all tried to do the same?

Okay, then, I hope you will consider these considerables and I wish you success, whatever that means for you, as you implement them in your life with passion, patience, and perseverance.

Thanks, rock on, and be kind to yourselves and each other.

Acknowledgements

This book comprises 40 of my favorite life lessons learned from many of the extraordinary people that I have been fortunate to encounter over the course of my life. Therefore, you can probably guess what's coming now. To everyone who has ever shared insights and/or taught me something that helped enhance my life and everyone to whom I've said or done something that taught them a lesson or two that made them feel better about themselves and/or their lives, thank you for sharing this journey.

And thanks to the following for their contributions to the creation of this book: My wonderful editor and friend, Nancy Cohen. My wise Rebbe, Rabbi Irwin Kula. Hank, Allison, Frank, Levon, Linda, Leon, and Craig for letting me share their stories. Colleen Sell, fellow writer and generous friend, for her eagle-eyed final review. My graphic designer and muse, FAB. My family and friends and co-workers and teachers (of all kinds) who have inspired me to try to do or write something to make this world a little bit better than it already is.

Thanks, thanks, thanks! Patience, persistence, and perseverance and love, love, love!

About the Author

Richard Krevolin is a graduate of Yale College who went on to earn a master's degree in screenwriting at UCLA's School of Cinema-Television and a master's degree in playwriting from USC. He has been an adjunct Professor of Dramatic Writing at USC School of Cinema/TV, UCLA, Pepperdine, Emerson, Ithaca College, University of Redlands, and The University of Georgia. Under his guidance, students have learned to structure and develop their screenplays and novels and even sold film scripts and TV shows to Universal, Sony-Tri-Star, Warner Brothers, Paramount, Dreamworks, and numerous other studios and production companies.

Krevolin is the author of the books *Screenwriting from the Soul* (St. Martin's Press), *Pilot Your Life* (Prentice-Hall), *How to Adapt Anything into a Screenplay* (Wiley & Sons), and *Screenwriting in the Land of Oz* (Adams Media/Writer's Digest Books).

He is also the writer of several young adult novels and over twenty stage plays, many of which have been produced throughout the US. He was one of the writers of the documentary *Fiddler on the Roof: 30 Years of Tradition* and then wrote and directed a documentary about theater during the Holocaust, *Making Light in Terezin,* which aired on PBS stations around the country. A companion book by the same title was also published containing entire interviews with the Holocaust survivors and others who were showcased in the film. And recently, he wrote and directed the feature film *Attachments,* starring Academy Award-

121

nominated actress Katharine Ross, which premiered at Worldfest Houston, where it won a special jury prize.

In addition to being a finalist for the $500,000 Kingman Screenwriting Award, the Chesterfield Contest, the Klasky-Csupo Writing for Children Contest, and the Nicholl Fellowship Screenwriting Award, Krevolin won the USC One-Act Play Festival for his comedy *Love Is Like Velcro*. His play *Trotsky's Garden* was a finalist for the Eugene O'Neill National Playwrights' Conference. His one-man show *Yahrzeit*, a finalist in the HBO New Writer's Project, was a huge hit at the Santa Monica Playhouse, running for five sold-out months. In 1997, under a new name, *Boychik*, it opened Off-Broadway at Theater Four in New York City and then toured the country. He also received a Valley Theatre League nomination for best director and best play for his one-man musical, *RebbeSoul-O*.

Another of Krevolin's plays, *King Levine*, opened at the Odyssey Theater under the direction of Joseph Bologna and, after receiving rave reviews, transferred to The Tiffany. It was also nominated for an Ovation Award as Best Adaptation. In 2001, two of his one-person plays opened in Los Angeles, *The Lemony Fresh Scent of Diva Monsoon Man* (starring Ruth DeSosa) at the Rose Alley and *Seltzer Man* (starring David Proval of *The Sopranos*) at the Tiffany. His plays have included performances by Ed Asner, Allan Arbus, Jean Smart, Mackenzie Phillips, and Richard Kline, among others. His Off-Broadway stage play, *Lansky*, was nominated for an Outer Critics Circle Award and was a hit at the National Yiddish Theater in Tel Aviv. Another play, *The Gospel According to*

Jerry, opened at the Minnesota Jewish Theater and then was produced across the country. *Sort of a Love Story*, which he wrote with Academy Award nominated writer Joe Bologna, was produced at the El Portal Theater in LA. In 2022, one of Krevolin's newer plays, *Our Town... but WILDER,* was produced Off-Broadway at the Actors Temple Theater and was nominated for the Broadway World Awards' "Best Production of a Play Off-Broadway" and "Best New Off-Broadway Play."

Over the past three decades, Professor Krevolin has flown around the world to teach the art of communication and storytelling to executives, creatives, and brand managers at many Fortune 100 companies. He continues to coach lawyers, writers, and brand executives privately as well as to lecture and lead creative workshops.

Rich Krevolin can be contacted at RKrevolin@Yahoo.com.